SERVICE NEWSPAPERS

SERVICE NEWSPAPERS OF THE SECOND WORLD WAR

Michael Anglo

JUPITER : LONDON

First published in 1977 by
JUPITER BOOKS (LONDON) LIMITED
167 Hermitage Road London N4 1LZ.

ISBN 0 904041 86 7

Composed in Photon Baskerville and
printed and bound in Great Britain by
R. J. Acford Limited, Industrial Estate, Chichester.

Contents

SERVICE
NEWSPAPERS
OF THE SECOND
WORLD WAR

No newspaper in wartime has unlimited freedom. We have the right of criticism and we exercise it. But if any serviceman imagines that a service newspaper can run a day-by-day 'campaign' against a considered Government or Service policy, irrespective of the factors that have dictated the policy, that serviceman is completely out of touch with reality. Such a situation does not exist in any service newspaper throughout the world.

Editor, *Seac*, V.E. issue, 9 May 1945

For Servicemen,
by Servicemen

WHATEVER shortages servicemen suffered overseas in World War II, they rarely lacked a regular supply of news and entertainment. Produced and distributed by the services, newspapers and magazines ranging from regular war-theatre publications such as *Parade*, the Middle East magazine, through the occasional regimental publication such as *Royal Fusiliers' Chronicle* to specialist magazines such as the fortnightly *Air Force Journal* and one-shot publications such as *IAF over Burma*, were to be found regularly in Naafis, messes, and welfare reading rooms, and were delivered with the rations by truck, plane, or parachute drop to troops in isolated or forward areas. Wherever British and American troops were serving together, they tended to read each other's service newspapers and periodicals. In South-East Asia they even produced a magazine, *Phoenix*, as a joint venture.

Such newspapers and magazines, produced by professional journalists and enthusiastic amateurs, were read diligently by soldiers, sailors, and airmen everywhere. Closely watched by the Establishment and often permeated with unsubtle propaganda, these newspapers and magazines provided a safety valve for the vast hordes of civilians in uniform who were enmeshed in the military machine. Liberally spiced with servicemen's argot, the vernacular of the particular service station, as well as formation and unit 'shop talk', they were, without a doubt, appreciated by all ranks. Humour, sport, short stories, poetry, and regular news items were all provided, mostly by the servicemen themselves. Editors gauged the mood of servicemen from readers' letters and carefully selected items for publication, airing views and grievances. Sometimes, by professing sympathy with disgruntled servicemen or by giving advice or taking up a cause, newspapers were able to defuse potentially explosive situations. Some editors stuck their necks out on occasion and were carpeted for their temerity.

Above all, service newspapers gave servicemen a sense of belonging, an identity and pride, yet provided a link with 'civvy street' to which they hoped to return one day. All service papers had their own particular stamp and appeal, often a reflection of the men who ran them and the command thinking behind them. This is well illustrated

Frank Owen, the talented journalist who became the first editor of *Seac*.

by a quotation from *Defeat into Victory* by Field-Marshal Sir William Slim, Commander of the Fourteenth Army in Burma. Referring to building the Fourteenth Army and providing for the welfare of the troops, he wrote:

An innovation was to be the publication of a theatre newspaper, *Seac*. One day I was told its editor designate was touring the Army area and had asked if I would see him. A hefty-looking second-lieutenant was ushered into my office and introduced as Frank Owen. I had strong views on Service Newspapers, and sat the young man down for ten minutes while I explained to him exactly how his paper should be run and what were an editor's duties. He listened very politely, and said he would do his best, saluted and left. It was only after he had gone that I learned he had been one of the youngest and most brilliant editors in Fleet Street and had characteristically thrown up his job to enlist at the beginning of the war. *Seac* under his direction – and Admiral Mountbatten wisely gave him complete editorial freedom – was the best wartime service journal I have ever seen. It – and Owen himself – made no mean contribution to our morale.

Frank Owen was a former international Rugby footballer who had won world fame by his brilliant editorship of Lord Beaverbrook's London *Evening Standard*. Of Welsh parentage, he had been educated at Monmouth Grammar School and Sidney Sussex College, Cambridge, before taking the plunge into provincial journalism. In 1929 he became the youngest Member of Parliament, representing Hereford. Failing to hold his seat in the election of 1931, he went to Fleet Street, where he worked for the *News Chronicle* and the *Daily Mirror* before going to the *Evening Standard* as assistant editor. Later, as editor, he established himself firmly as a leader of opinions.

From March until May 1942, Frank Owen cabled from London a fortnightly feature, 'News Headlights', to *Victory*, the weekly magazine for the India Command published in Calcutta. As editor of *Seac*, first published, with a print run of only 7,000, on Monday, 10 January 1944, when it was hailed as a newspaper in battledress, 2nd Lieutenant Owen, R.A.C., used to range far and wide, hardly ever wearing his badges of rank even when promoted to lieutenant-colonel, and meeting the top brass in the Allied services. Tough, resourceful, and uninhibited, Owen never pulled his punches. His able assistants included Lieut. Ian Coster from the London *Evening Standard*, Telegraphist Len Jackson, and George Chisholm from the *Sketch*.

Service newspapers and magazines, often produced under trying conditions and with whatever material was to hand, came in all shapes and sizes, from the large *Picture Post* format of *Parade*, the Middle East weekly which was first published in Cairo in August 1940, with subsequent editions in Polish, Arabic, Greek, and Turkish, to the Lilliputian *Victory*. Some were well produced and on good-

This toothsome pair decorate the large-format *Parade*.

PARADE

R.S.M.
"SOMEWHERE
IN SYRIA"

MIDDLE EAST WEEKLY	Chasing Battles with a Microphone	15 mills
JUNE 28, 1941	NO. 46, VOL. 4	20 MILS IN PALESTINE

quality paper; some were crude and produced on duplicating machines; some were printed on the presses of large, established newspapers under good conditions; others were printed on whatever presses were available, often under severe handicaps. Hugh Cudlipp, who became editor of *Union Jack*, and later was a force to be reckoned with in Fleet Street, even managed to produce a newspaper aboard an outward bound troopship.

When *Seac* was transferred to Singapore after the Japanese surrender in August 1945, it was printed on the presses of the *Straits Times*.

Serious and informative,
Ceylon Review's policy was
not only to entertain.

CEYLON
REVIEW

No. 15--Vol. V

October 7,
1944

F a l l
o f
Paris

●

'Boats'
over
B u r m a

●

Japan
Is
Next

Ceylon's Weekly Journal
the Royal Navy, Ar
R. A. F., Merchant N
and Civil Defence Servi

These had suffered a battering at the hands of the Japanese during the occupation, and the run-down machines were without spare parts. Yet despite this and shortages of printing inks and paper, the famous newspaper appeared every afternoon, perhaps not in the format to which the troops had become accustomed, but still the distinctive newspaper it had been from its inception. From the same presses, during the Japanese occupation, had come the *Syonan Shimbum*, a single-sheet newspaper in English that had been sponsored by the Japanese military.

Fauji Akhbar ('Soldiers' Newspaper'), a magazine published by Public Relations Directorate: G.H.Q. (India) in Delhi for Indian servicemen, had a wide circulation stretching from Persia and the North West Frontier to Burma and Ceylon. A strong feature of the magazine was sport, particularly boxing. Exploits of Indian regiments such as those of the Madrassis, Mahrattas, Rajputs, Gurkhas and Punjabis in the Middle East, Italy, and Greece, as well as in Burma, were recounted. The daily radio programmes for troops in India and Ceylon were given, with details of special music for N.W.F. soldiers, Maharastas, South India soldiers, and Gurkhas. There was also a modicum of home news as well as advertisements. The magazine was in English, the language understood by most Indian troops whatever their native tongue, be it Hindi, Gujerati, or Pushtu. Dogras, Jats, Baluchis, and Garwhalis, they all read *Fauji Akhbar. Bahut Achchha!*

Another newspaper published by the Indian G.H.Q., New Delhi, but printed in Ceylon, was *Contact*, a bi-weekly for British servicemen in India and Ceylon. The format was similar to that of *Seac*.

Ceylon Review, printed by the *Ceylon Observer Press* in Colombo for the publisher, Chief Public Relations Officer, Commander-in-Chief's office, Ceylon, was a weekly journal for Royal Navy, Army, R.A.F., Merchant Navy, and Civil Defence personnel. It carried a variety of features of a high standard, covering all theatres of war, all branches of the services, and all aspects of servicemen's interests – cultural, political, and aesthetic.

Admiral Sir Geoffrey Layton, Commander-in-Chief, Ceylon, had wanted a magazine for the fighting services in Ceylon. On 3 October 1942, the first issue of *Ceylon Review* appeared. The object of the magazine, as stated by the Admiral, was 'to give information and to encourage discussion; to inform about the war in all theatres and to give servicemen details of the world being planned for them'. On Layton's recall to the U.K., almost three years later, the editor stated that the sole aim and purpose of the magazine remained the same, hence the lack of 'indulgence in the fripperies of entertainment'.

Ceylon Review's information ranged from articles about Ceylon itself and countries further east, to, later, details of all the post-war planning that was taking place at home. Material for discussion was provided by articles whose widely divergent points of view ranged from *The Times* to the *Daily Worker*, written by people such as Quintin Hogg, Harry Pollit, and Hannen Swaffer. The many contributors to *Ceylon*

Review included Emmanuel Shinwell, Lady Violet Bonham Carter, Bertrand Russell, J. B. Priestley, Eduard Benes, Wickham Steed, and Willi Frischauer. In addition there were articles, excerpts, and stories reprinted from American publications such as the *New Yorker* and the *Saturday Evening Post* as well as from *Pravda* and other foreign publications, plus selected items from other service publications.

Tobruk Truth, a paper produced in February 1941 during the siege of Tobruk with news based on B.B.C. broadcasts, was described by Warwick Charlton, later editor of *The Crusader* and *Eighth Army News*, as the father of Desert newspapers. During the siege a competition was held for the best poem, the prize being a precious bottle of beer. An Australian lieutenant was the winner and his poem was later reprinted in *Parade* in September 1941. It was called 'Ode to the Best Beloved' and naturally was about a bottle of beer.

The Crusader, an English army weekly issued to the fighting forces in the Desert, made its first appearance on 2 May 1942.

Jambo, published in Nairobi, Kenya, by the General Staff Branch (Intelligence) H.Q., East Africa Command, was a magazine for the three services in the command and for troops from East Africa serving outside the command. Reminding service readers that the magazine was non-profit-making and that service contributors could not be paid, the editor urged artists and writers to send in their offerings nevertheless, as the magazine was an excellent opportunity to bring their talents to the fore and was a 'shop window' for post-war careers. Whether the carrot was tempting or not, servicemen's contributions were never lacking. *Jambo* was completely run by service personnel. In February 1944, for example, the editor was a captain, N. A. C. Tyfield; the assistant editor, a S.Q.M.S., H. Myers; the art editor, a sergeant, J. S. Spiers; and the business manager, another sergeant, D. Green. Captain Tyfield, as well as editing the magazine, often wrote features. The magazine, in small format, comprised sixty-eight pages and was profusely illustrated with line drawings and cartoons. Few of the features were serious, but those that were, were informative and often sharply pointed. Poems and readers' letters were popular features of *Jambo*, and soldiers' Kiswahili of the area was often a colourful decoration. *Nine jembe*!

Service newspapers and magazines were, for the most part, issued free to servicemen, although some were paid for from service welfare funds. Magazines and newspapers with a distribution among troops in and around large towns, accessible to off-duty servicemen and men on leave, often carried advertising, and this was a source of revenue which helped considerably in paying for a publication's production. Both *Jambo* and *Review*, the East African Command's more serious fortnightly which replaced the more modest *Off Parade* in February 1944, carried a quota of advertisements.

In *Jambo*, Torr's Hotel advertised dinner dances and stated, 'No admittance to the Ball Room unless accompanied by a Lady Partner or be in a party with a Lady Partner.' Another frequent advertiser

stated, 'From Cape Town to Cairo, the Favourite Rendezvous of the Forces is the Free French Restaurant, Chez Gaby, Nairobi.' Cars, beer, whisky, restaurants, books, equipment outfitters, and tailors were advertised in *Jambo*; but when it came to tailors, no service publication, or indeed any other, for that matter, could match *Battle Dress*, the O.C.T.U. magazine published in Aldershot. In the February 1940 issue, for example, out of twenty pages of advertising eighteen were for tailors and outfitters. One advertiser was Moss Bros. It is said

BATTLE DRESS

THE CADET MAGAZINE

No. 2   February, 1940   Price 1/-

that a cadet passing out in March 1940 hired an outfit from Moss Bros. and exchanged it in 1946 for a dinner suit to celebrate his demob.

Cinemas found service publications useful for advertising their shows, and service pages often featured appeals, requests for information, and welfare information too. In issue 16 of *Union Jack* in 1944, there was a strange boxed appeal for refrigerators in which to store blood for transfusions. As soon as Rome was occupied, *Union Jack* carried a map of Rome showing canteens and welfare centres.

The first number of *Union Jack*, which was amalgamated with *Eighth Army News*, was published in Tunis for the B.N.A.F. by the British Army Newspaper Unit on Wednesday, 22 September 1943, as the Third African Edition. Maj. Hugh Cudlipp was editor-in-chief, and K. C. Harvey editor. Printed on the presses of the *Tunis Telegraph*, *Union Jack* appeared three times a week at first, but soon became the 'Daily Newspaper for the British Fighting Services'. The Constantine edition was published from 3 November 1943. Then with the invasion of Sicily and Italy came the various Italian editions such as the Western and Eastern Italy editions, and a Central Italy edition to serve areas further forward than those normally supplied by the Western Italy edition was published by the Newspapers Unit, C.M.F. With the British intervention in Greece against E.L.A.S. came a Greek edition of *Union Jack* from 22 January 1945.

Features in the newspaper included sports commentaries and short stories by Peter Wilson, 'Show Parade' by Isadore Green, and 'Now We're Talking' by Bernard Brett, a lance-corporal. Another feature was a daily Italian lesson. Short stories by popular humorous writers such as George Maracco, who wrote a series called 'My Girl Effie' for *London Opinion*, were reprinted from home publications from time to time, as well as articles by political and military commentators.

Headlines and news stories in *Union Jack* were bold and punchy. The day after the Allies took Naples, *Union Jack* headlines proclaimed: 'Allies in Naples – Fleeing Nazis loot, burn, stricken city.' A salutary reminder to the troops of the nature of the enemy was a front-page story by Anthony Eden about the mass escape from a German P.O.W. camp, Stalag Luft III, as a result of which fifty British and Allied air force officers were shot by the Germans. 'It was clear', declared Eden, 'that these officers were murdered.'

Sometimes service newspapers were first with the news, as with the announcement that the 78th Division had joined the Eighth Army at the beginning of the campaign then in progress, and had played a prominent part in the advance from 120 miles south-east of Rome to 180 miles north of the capital, crossing the Rapido and encircling Cassino.

Front-page news in *Union Jack* in July 1944 announced that, in Italy, the King was paying his fourth visit to a war zone. His first had been to France in 1939 when he toured the Maginot Line, the next when he had gone to Malta and North Africa in June 1943,

21

and his third in June 1944 when he had visited Montgomery's H.Q. in Normandy.

Sometimes a newspaper drew attention to the more unsavoury aspects of the services, perhaps with a view to 'encourage the others'. In October 1945, *Seac* published an item from a British parish magazine about 'British Concentration Camps' for the detention of British army personnel. Under the headline 'Dark Secrets of the Glass House', the item read as follows:

> 'Infamous happenings' at Takehill Military Detention Camp near Rochdale are alleged by the curate of the neighbouring parish of St Martin's, Castleton, the Rev. Urien Evans, writing in the parish magazine.
>
> He writes: 'Castleton is becoming infamous. For some weeks the new vicar and I have been taking services for 400 British Church of England soldiers at the detention barracks.
>
> 'Some of the things that go on there would no doubt surprise and pain the people of Castleton, but they knew nothing about it.
>
> 'The people of Germany were held morally responsible for what went on in their concentration camps. Can we be morally responsible for the dark and well-veiled secrets of the "glass house"?'
>
> The Camp Commandant, Lt.-Col. Pavey, would not comment to the Press nor would he confirm or deny rumours that, recently, two military prisoners attempted suicide.
>
> Soldiers are sent from all parts of the North of England to serve sentences at the camp in an old mill, midway between Rochdale and Manchester.
>
> The curate would not add to the written statement beyond saying that the vicar edited and passed the matter appearing in the parish magazine.
>
> The Western Command Public Relations section stated, 'We have had no complaints from that area.'

Authentic battle stories and battle cameos were frequent features in service publications. Typical was the following from September 1944, under the headline 'Steve Roberts sends these shoots to *Union Jack* from the Italian battlefield' in a series entitled 'Up Front in Italy'.

> A large house with a central courtyard stood near the Canal Naviglione two miles north of Bagnavacavallo. In one end were Germans, in the other Canadians including a gunner officer.
>
> The gunner solved the trouble of the unsuited neighbours by calling down a stonk which demolished the German end of the building. Nine Jerries transferred to our wing.
>
> While the roof blazed as the result of a direct hit from a shell the I.Q.'s room on the ground floor of a farmhouse occupied by Brigade H.Q. was turned into a maternity yard. Two Canuck

Directed at new cadets, this Moss Bros. advertisement for well-cut uniforms appeared in *Battle Dress*.

drivers delivered a lusty son to an Italian woman. The baby was named John after the 'A' and 'Q' majors.

Two Panthers and a Tiger seen nose to tail from an O.P. near Bagnavacavallo made a party for three Canadian officers, Captain Don Smith, M.C., infantry commander, and two Artyfoos, Captain Pete Newell, M.C., and Captain William Godfrey.

Hitching a six-pounder to a jeep they hunted the three tanks and say the one that got away was the 'biggest ever'.

A .50 machine-gun firing from 30 yards can do a lot of damage.

23

UNION JACK

FOR THE BRITISH FIGHTING FORCES

Monday, July 31, 1944
No 42 Two Lire

STOP PRESS

REPORTED LATE YESTERDAY THAT BRITISH TANKS AND INFANTRY ACHIEVED THEIR FIRST OBJECTIVES IN CAUMONT AREA ON WIDE FRONT FROM CAUMONT EASTWARDS. CHURCHILL TANKS REPORTED IN ACTION.

AT THE GATES OF WARSAW

STRIKING at the ever-retreating Germans with a speed and ferocity unequalled in modern warfare, the armies of Generals Rokossovsky and Koniev have reached the outskirts of Warsaw and have brought artillery to bear on the outer defences. Direct assault on the defenders of the city is imminent.

Over the week-end considerable progress was made in other sectors. Brest-Litovsk, Kaunas, Przemysl and Yaroslav have all been captured, and in the advance on Riga the Russians are only a day's march from the Baltic.

Summing up the great German retreat "The Times" says: "The German Armies, reeling backwards from the ruins of their enterprise in Russia, approach every day to a catastrophe surpassing that of 1813."

Last night correspondents said that Marshal Rokossovsky had established his headquarters on the outskirts of the Polish capital and that the German High Command had ordered the Warsaw garrison to "fight for every house, every heap of rubble."

At the point where the Russians crossed the Vistula, the last natural barrier for at least 100 miles to the west, they were 140 miles from the German frontier and 200 miles from Breslau and vital Silesia.

Brest-Litovsk was liquidated several days after Russian by-passing armies had reached the Vistula. It was the first large city to fall to the Germans when they attacked Russia in 1941 and was the scene of the bitter and merciless peace treaty with the Germans in 1917.

West of the town three enemy divisions were encircled and pressed to the River Bug, where they are being reduced.

Przemysl and Yaroslav, both on the west bank of the River San, 17 miles apart, fell when the San was forced by troops of the First Ukrainian Front. Przemysl is a key communications centre and an important stepping stone to Cracow, towards which Russian columns are now moving.

Advancing into the Baltic States, the Russians are making rapid progress towards the sea. General Bagramyan's forces have entered southern Latvia and are driving on Jelgava railway junction, only 23 miles south of Riga.

The German news agency reported the loss of Kaunas, but its capture has not yet been announced by the Russians.

The military correspondent of "The Times" writes: Although progress generally by the Russians is being maintained in almost every sector from Narva to the Carpathians, there are three clearly-defined movements—1. to cut off the 20-30 German divisions in the Baltic, now in its last stages; 2, to take Warsaw, and thence across central Poland to Berlin; 3, to drive along the Carpathians to Silesia.

Polish PM to see Stalin

THE Polish Prime Minister, Stanislaw Mikolajczyk, has arrived in Teheran on his way to Moscow to see Marshal Stalin.

According to the "Observer," Mikolajczyk is prepared to go all the way towards meeting Soviet demands on the frontier question, and will express his Government's willingness to accept the Curzon Line as a temporary demarcation between Poland and Russia.

He will also propose, says the newspaper, the transfer of the seat of the Polish Government to Warsaw immediately after its liberation by the Soviet armies, and on its arrival there the Government would reconstruct itself according to the wishes of the Polish people.

Welcoming the journey to Moscow of the Polish Premier, "The Times" says that his political record in Poland as leader of the large Peasant Party and his balanced approach to all problems make him a good spokesman.

DEAT AND LAVAL FALL OUT

Marcel Deat, Vichy Minister of Labour, is openly at loggerheads with Laval, reports Reuter, and in an open letter has declared that preparations for evacuating the people of Normandy from the war zone are a public disgrace.

The letter added that Deat was going to put all the facts of the Vichy Government's procrastination and indecision before the public at a mass meeting in the Salle Wagram in Paris.

Deat demanded dictatorial powers to over-rule all police and prefectorial decisions. Laval's reply was to order the Paris police to occupy the Salle Wagram and prohibit the meeting. He told Deat that he objected to such matters being discussed in public.

AVIATION TALKS

Lord Beaverbrook, who heads the British oil delegation now in the US, has authority to continue Anglo-American discussions on post-war international aviation, the Prime Minister told the House of Commons.

8th close in on Florence

EIGHTH ARMY forces are closing in on Florence in the face of stubborn resistance and fierce counter-attacks, which have been repelled with heavy losses to the enemy.

Following the Eighth Army's break-through on July 28 it has become increasingly obvious that the enemy is determined to hold the last hill line south of the city.

The official communique states that to the west of Florence troops of an Indian division of the Eighth Army in their advance to the River Arno are now in the outskirts of Empoli and are approaching Montelupo. Local but important gains have been made on both banks of the river in the Upper Arno Valley.

Montelupo is situated at the junction of the Pesa with the Arno, and our troops are within two miles of the outskirts. New Zealanders withstood a second counter-attack at midday on July 28 and are standing firm in their positions across the Pesa.

Positions regained

During the night they regained two positions lost in the counter-attacks and reached San Michele.

The enemy is reacting strongly to any penetrations in this sector and made another counter-attack on Saturday but without success. German forces have been brought from farther west to strengthen the troops astride Highway Two.

In the mountains west of Highway 69 our infantry have pushed along the hilltop and reached Monte Scalari, the highest point in the high ground south of Florence.

West of Figline Eighth Army troops pushed on 2,000 yards and captured a 1,700-foot hill. Patrols entered Castelfranco, which was found to be unoccupied. Persignano was passed as the battle became more fluid in this difficult sector.

North-east of Arezzo the enemy has pulled his forces back to the next hill line three miles farther north.

After fierce fighting the town and road centre of Anghiari, which was strongly defended, was captured. The enemy is giving the impression of thinning slightly in this area, but contact is being maintained.

There were no changes in the Adriatic or Fifth Army sectors.

GERMAN LOSSES

SINCE the Allied offensive began on May 11, the German armies in Italy have lost at least 250 tanks, 360 assault guns, 450 heavy anti-tank guns and 650 other artillery pieces, it was officially announced yesterday.

The number of tanks destroyed represents 75 per cent. of the establishment of two armoured divisions and includes a high proportion of "Panthers" and "Tigers." The total of field and medium guns captured or destroyed would be sufficient to equip nine German divisions.

Enemy mines explode near the King

TWO German mines were exploded less than 300 yards from the King at lunch. Seated with the King were Lieut.-General Mark Clark and other British and American military leaders, and Archbishop Spellman of New York.

The American soldier who inadvertently set off the mines was killed instantly. No-one of the King's party was injured. He had just finished inspecting a parade of American troops when the incident happened.

After his visit to the Eighth Army, the King spent a day visiting airfields and reviewing troops of the Fifth Army. He was accompanied by Lieut.-General Clark, by whom he was greeted on arrival at an advanced airfield (picture). His Majesty was also met by Air Vice-Marshal Dickson, Air Officer Commanding Desert Air Force, and subsequently inspected a number of RAF squadrons of the Force.

His Majesty proceeded to review troops representing the various combat and service branches of the Fifth Army, including infantry, artillery, engineers, armour, anti-aircraft, WACs, nurses and air OP personnel.

On arrival at General Clark's Command Post, His Majesty conferred the Cross of Honorary Knight of the British Empire upon General Clark, the Cross of Honorary Companion of the Bath on Major-General Alfred M. Grunther, Chief of General Staff, Fifth Army, and on Major-General Keyes, commanding the US II Corps.

British launch fresh attack in Normandy

A NEW British attack, preceded by a large-scale air bombardment, was launched in the vicinity of Caumont, almost half-way between St. Lo and Villers Bocage, early yesterday morning. No details of progress have yet been reported. News from the American sector of the front continues to be of progress in all areas, and a Reuter report from SHAEF says the Germans are now withdrawing from all points west of St. Lo.

Yesterday's SHAEF communique said that Allied forces pushing south from Coutances have linked up with other troops in Legronne, and the whole of the lateral road between these two towns is now in our hands. An enemy force south of the Soulles River has been surrounded, and is being steadily eliminated in spite of determined efforts to break out.

William Steen, Reuter's Special Correspondent at SHAEF, says American armoured columns which captured Coutances on Friday went on to advance six miles beyond the town along the road leading south to Granville the following day. The capture of Coutances effectively cuts off any German troops still to the north of the town, but it is believed that the bulk of them made an orderly withdrawal.

One German E-boat was sunk and several others damaged by British light coastal forces in an encounter with a heavy enemy force off the Normandy coast, an Admiralty communique stated.

Throughout Saturday Allied fighters and fighter-bombers closely supported our advancing troops.

Reports from France during the week-end say Rommel (on right) has been seriously wounded on a visit to the front.

Canadian VC

A CANADIAN Flight-Lieutenant, David Ernest Hornell, has been awarded the Victoria Cross posthumously.

He is the first Canadian airman to win the VC in this war. He became blind and died after 21 hours in a dinghy when his plane crashed in the sea following a successful attack on a U-boat.

The citation said: "By pressing home a skilful and successful attack against fierce opposition, and by fortifying and encouraging his comrades in their subsequent ordeal, this officer displayed valour and devotion to duty of the highest order"

Other decorations are being awarded to members of his crew.

NO PENSIONS NOW

The Italian Government has ordered the stoppage of State pensions payable to Italians who fought as volunteers in Spain.

VAST REFORM PLANS FOR INDIA

GIVING renewed assurances that the British Government stands by its promises of independence to India after the war, Mr. L. S. Amery, Secretary for India, has announced in the House of Commons a big reform programme for the country.

While conditions for a political solution were maturing, reforms were to be pushed ahead for doubling the agricultural capacity of the country over the next fifteen years, providing a universal compulsory free education at a cost rising to 800,000,000 pounds, and for building 400,000 miles of roads. India, he said, stood on the eve of a great industrial advance.

During the subsequent debate several speakers suggested that a move should be made to resume discussions on an agreement.

A Reuter message from Lahore says that Jinnah, President of the Moslem League, has accepted Gandhi's proposal that the two should meet. The meeting may take place in Bombay some time next week.

And when a strong party of Boche, launching a counter attack north of Ravenna, ran into withering fire from one of these 'fifties' and a smaller calibre machine-gun, both of which were mounted on a jeep, they did the wisest thing and dived for the nearest cover, a river bank.

But behind this jeep were five others, all equally heavily armed, and when the first ran out of ammo another took its place.

And so it went on. Every time a Boche poked his head up a stream of metal shot at him across the river. Even the German machine-gunners on their flanks found it disastrous to try a burst.

The Germans came no further than the river, and when our patrols crossed later they found the evidence of their marksmanship – 30 bodies.

Personalities, civil and military, made the news in service papers as frequently as they did in the national press. *Seac* ran a column called 'People'. When Eddie Rickenbacker, the famous American air ace of World War I, was overdue on a flight between Oahu, Hawaii, and another Pacific island, it was reported in *Stars and Stripes*. News of sporting and film celebrities in and out of uniform appeared regularly in service newspapers and magazines. Charlie Chaplin came in for a drubbing in American service newspapers in the course of 1945. *C.B.I. Roundup*, the weekly newspaper of the United States forces, published 'by the men for the men' in China, Burma, and India, had this to say about Charles Chaplin under the headline ' "It's a smear," says Chaplin of charges':

> Referring to the demand of Rep. William Langer (R.N.D.) that he be deported from the country because he is a menace to public morals and had not sought U.S. citizenship ... Despite his seeming reluctance to apply for U.S. citizenship, Chaplin has no scruples about using American mediums and territory for a self-announced new picture, *Monsieur Bluebeard* ... Chaplin claimed that 65 per cent of his revenue came from abroad and added that the U.S. Government enjoys full taxes on that 65 per cent and on the 35 per cent he earned in the U.S.A.

Lili Pons and Andre Kostelanetz were given full coverage for their concert tour of the China, India, Burma theatre where, according to *Roundup*, they had a terrific reception. The results of a Gallup poll were also published showing that the favourite movie of 1944 had been *Going My Way*, and Bing Crosby had won an Oscar for his performance in it. The movie, of course, had gone the rounds of American bases. U.S. personnel were always shown the latest movies and Bing Crosby always had a good press.

In South-East Asia the cantankerous, tough American general Joe Stilwell, who commanded American and Chinese troops in North Burma and was responsible for the building of the Ledo Road between China and Burma after the closing of the Burma Road, often made

Union Jack; a precursor of the post-war *Daily Mirror* under Maj. Hugh Cudlipp.

WORST WEEK OF WAR FOR JAPANESE AS NAZI WESTERN FRONT CITIES BURN

Reds Renounce Neutrality Pact; Koiso Junked

Roundup Staff Article

As the war's worst week for Japan ended, representatives of 30 United Nations opened a Pre-Conference session of the San Francisco Security meeting this week in a clarified atmosphere brought about by the Soviet Union's denunciation of its five-year Neutrality Pact with Nippon.

The Soviet action drew a flood of favorable U.S. comment. Almost gone were the suspicions engendered by the Soviet demand for three votes in the proposed assembly and recognition of the Warsaw-based Government as the sole representative of Poland at the Security Conference.

Speculation that the Soviet Union was not too interested in the outcome of the Security meeting had vanished. The U. S. still refused to recognize the Warsaw (Lublin) Government as representing Poland at San Francisco but Secretary of State Edward Stettinius stated work was continuing to bring the Soviet-sponsored and London Poles together for a representative delegation for their country.

Stettinius also said that the U.S. would not ask for three votes in the assembly to balance the Soviet request. Sen. Arthur Vandenberg (R.-Mich.), leading Republican on the U.S. delegation, said he felt the American group is "morally bound" by the President's promise at Yalta to back the Soviet request for three votes, although the Senator has personally condemned multiple voting for any country.

The U. S. delegation is holding conferences to determine its stand on policy questions likely to be brought up at the Conference. One is Vandenberg's proposal that the projected peace-keeping league have the power to review war time decisions on boundaries.

It is believed that a statement by Stettinius shortly after his

(Continued on page 11, Col. 1.)

ARMY TO WAIT UNTIL V-E DAY ON 'POINTS'

WASHINGTON. — (ANS) — The Army is adhering to a policy of waiting until V-E Day to determine the value of point credits upon which soldiers will be discharged, the *Associated Press* declared this week.

The finally determined total point score will be used in selecting personnel to be discharged after being declared surplus, AP said.

The War Department originally announced four factors for determining priority of discharge: (1) service credit, (2) overseas service, (3) combat, (4) parenthood, AP declared.

Service credit will be granted on the total number of months of service since Sept. 16, 1940, and overseas credit on the number of months overseas, AP added.

The *Associated Press* story did not comment upon the combat and parenthood credit factors.

"The mere possession of sufficient credits, however, is no guarantee that the soldier will be discharged," AP said. "Certain types of personnel will not be declared surplus until Japan is defeated.

"The Army, for instance, has said that service troops will be needed in the very first phases of redeployment to prepare bases in the Pacific, and the Air Forces have announced that many, perhaps most, of the air ground crews will be hurried to the Pacific after V-E Day," the AP story concluded.

INDIA - BURMA THEATER

Roundup

Vol. III No. 31.   Delhi, Thursday, April 12, 1945.   Reg. No. L5015

Third Army Seizes All Nazi Gold

PARIS—(ANS)—Gen. George Patton's Third Army has captured all the gold in Germany. And that isn't all.

The onrushing Third seized an underground storehouse containing 100 tons of gold bullion and currency and art treasures valued at billions of dollars. The Nazi gold reserve and other treasure was found in a salt mine at Merkers, 25 miles southwest of Gotha. The currency store included $2,000,000 of American money.

Reichsbank officials said that the bullion was all the gold in Germany and that it had taken five weeks to move the vast treasure from Berlin. Billions in currency of other nations, originals by Raphael, Van Dyke, and Durer, and 120 cases of Goethe's original manuscripts were found.

From Washington came word that as far as the U.S. was concerned it was "finders keepers."

PLAN SCHOOLS FOR ETO G.I.'S

WASHINGTON — (UP) — United States troops will go to school while waiting passage homeward or to Asia, the War Department said here this week.

It is expected that it will take many months to transfer soldiers from Europe, and the program—ranging from sixth grade through second year college—will be stressed in order to prevent those months from being wasted time.

Opportunities may be given to attend foreign universities, it was also announced.

I-B Sets World Mark In Unloading Ships

Roundup Staff Article

The India-Burma Theater unloaded ships faster than anywhere else in the world during the month of February.

As a result the percentage of idle port time for vessels during that month was less than that of any other Theater in the Army.

This Theater led its closest rival during that month in everything relating to vessel utilization by 100% or more.

Authority for these statements is Maj. Gen. W. E. R. Covell, Commanding General of Services of Supply for this Theater.

NO MYSTERY

The SOS chief says there is no mystery as to the cause of this productive record. He explains it as a natural result of efficiency, speed, determination, and consistent effort on the part of the Army personnel who work and manage the Indian coolies.

One G.I. explained it very simply:

"We do our job in the best possible way. Our paths are not crossed by wild animals. We don't have to crawl on our bellies into foxholes with snakes. We don't have to live in disease infested jungles. But we do worry about the G.I.'s who are up there in Burma and China doing just that and we don't intend to let them down."

WORK BEFORE DOCKING

One reason for the Calcutta efficiency is explained by a ship unloading operation that recently took place. The Transportation Corps soldiers boarded the vessel en route to the dock in a short canal emptying into the Hooghly River.

The men began to unloosen the cables which held the deck cargo consisting of a large number of Army trucks. In other words the men make a practice of starting their work even before the ship is tied up.

BEAT OWN SCHEDULE

On this same ship when the Army men told the crew the time in which they proposed to have the cargo ashore, they were met with incredulous smiles. But

(Continued on page 11, Col. 4.)

Ding Dong Daddy Gets 30 Years, Small Fine For Bigamy Activity

SAN FRANCISCO.— (ANS) — Francis Van Wie, the strange moon-faced little street car conductor and husband of 13 wives, was sentenced to 30 years in San Quentin prison and fined $3 here this week.

The erstwhile ding-dong daddy of the carbarns, variously a circus barker and lion tamer, said he married so often because "all I sought was happiness. All I wanted was a pal."

Van Wie pleaded not guilty by reason of insanity. He said he had been kicked in the head by a mule, fallen off a ladder, and suffered other injuries which impaired his brain.

The slight fine imposed was to conform to a statutory provision of the penal code.

THE EYEFUL

Meet Adele Jergens, Columbia Pictures newest glamor recruit. Miss Jergens came to the movies via modeling, ballet, and the theater. Some of the boys down Kandy way did us this favor.

Allied Columns Head For Elbe; Patton Puzzle

Roundup Staff Article.

German cities in the path of the advancing Allied armies on the Western Front were masses of flames this week; more than half a million Germans were casualties since April 1; U.S. and British tanks were heading for the Elbe River, only 50 miles from Berlin.

Such was this week's picture on the chaotic Western Front where the American and British Armies were daily cutting off more segments of the scattered Nazi Army, while penetrating and threatening more arsenal cities.

The progress of Lt. Gen. George Patton's Third U.S. Army has been buried in security silence most of the week. Patton's troops were last reported as the closest to a junction with the Soviet armies and also as the closest to Berlin. *Army News Service's* last figure put Patton 57 miles from the Czech border, 110 miles from Berlin, and about 165 miles from a junction with the Soviets.

In the meantime, the Canadians had cut off most of the German troops in Holland, aided by paratroops, who were

(Continued on page 11, Col. 5.)

VINSON QUIET ON CHANGING WAR EDICTS

Roundup Staff Article

Key figure of the home front in reconversion to peace time industry will be Fred M. Vinson, who this week took the oath as successor to James Byrnes as Director of War Mobilization after being confirmed unanimously by the Senate.

Speculation immediately started as to whether Vinson would ease up the nationwide curfew and lift the ban on horse racing. There is nothing in the law that says he cannot change the policies laid down by Byrnes.

HAS LOAN JOB TOO

Byrnes, who has returned to private life following his resignation last week, said in his final report that the restrictions would be eased after the fall of Germany. Vinson had no immediate comment on any of the policies that brought Byrnes criticism from various pressure groups.

Vinson was Economic Stabilization Director, then resigned to accept the Loan Administrator post left vacant after the "Dear Jesse" letter of President Roosevelt to Jesse Jones, which resulted in the exit of the conservative Texan from both his Commerce and Loan posts. Vinson still retains the Loan Administrator job along with his new post as War Mobilizer.

BROWNOUT LIFT

In the meantime, the War Production Board announced the brownout has been lifted in Maine. This has nothing except local significance, however, as Maine exists on water power and there would be no saving of fuel during the summer. Wyoming, Nevada, and Colorado are also being considered by the WPB as they use slack coal, not used in the fuel-starved East.

And in Toledo, O., a strike threat by the motion pictures operators union ended the one man rebellion of theater owner Jack O'Connell against the midnight curfew. The operators refused to allow their men to work after midnight anymore, and where O'Connell refused to bow to the Federal Government, he capitulated to the union.

the news in service newspapers and the national press alike. Known
as Vinegar Joe or Uncle Joe, he was forever shooting off his mouth
and had the rank and, as often as not, the reason to do so. There
were many stories about him, apocryphal and otherwise. In June
1944, an editorial in *Seac* started:

> Uncle Joe Stilwell sucks on his lip, cocks his head, shoots
> you his quick half-mocking glance thro' the steel-rimmed
> spectacles. He says:
> 'I once had officers on my staff named Ryder, Reeder and
> Radar. I raked thro' the Army List to get two more – Roder and
> Ruder, but no luck. Now take General Pick, who's building
> the road there. If only I could find him a Major Shovel.'
> The 'road there' is the Ledo Road that Stilwell's mind
> planned. Pick's is the hand that built it.

Servicemen were made familiar with the faces of their leaders,
as well as with their antics and gimmicks. British and U.S. troops
were as familiar with the flashy yet meticulous dress of General
Patton as they were with the 'informal' dress of General Montgomery.
Through service newspapers they heard of Patton's disgusting treatment
of a wounded soldier in Italy and of Montgomery's 'knock 'em for
six' speech in the Western Desert.

Magazines such as *Parade* and *Yank* carried many photographs and
photographic features. Pin-ups and photos of film stars clipped from
publications such as these adorned the walls of billets and ward
rooms from the Aleutians to Africa. Betty Grable of the fabulous

An eyeful before the Roundup.

27

Soldier, Can You Pick the Prize Beauty Here?

LEMME SEE.... Somewhere in this group of eleven beauties at Atlantic City, N. J., is Miss America. Can you find her? Well, then, now look at the picture at bottom right on this page. There you see the winner, Jo-Carroll Dennison from "Deep in the Heart of Texas"—Tyler, to be exact. In photo above she stands second from right.

Billet adornments from *Yank*.

legs, sweater girl Lana Turner, sarong-clad Dorothy Lamour, and swimsuited Esther Williams were favourites with servicemen everywhere.

Servicemen were given their full quota of sports coverage. Peter Wilson wrote a column, 'Sports Talking', for *Union Jack*; and George Chisholm wrote regularly for *Seac*. Sports writers were always optimistic about the prospects for sport after the war, and inter-services boxing and football were reported and encouraged. News of sportsmen in and out of the forces, horse-racing, and developments in sport at home were regularly reported. In the *Union Jack* of 10 November 1944, Peter Wilson wrote: 'Elvin plans a Super Wembley. He intends to promote ice hockey, indoor athletics, six-day cycle races, professional lawn tennis, boxing, table tennis and championship swimming as he did before the war.'

Wherever servicemen operated, service publications were started. *Crete News*, produced in Canea, was the first British paper published in Crete. When the British moved into Madagascar in 1942 and occupied the capital, Diego Suarez, the *Evening Pioneer* appeared as the first British daily paper. It was followed by the *Morning Pioneer*,

Making somebody's Christmas: more pin-ups from *Yank*.

Hollywood's Christmas Crackers

Everything in Hollywood is laid on with a trowel, from glorious technicolour to Christmas whimsy. This Christmas the Star in the East has inspired the stars in the West to pull out some of their oddest camera tricks. Showing a grim determination to live up to the "Let Nothing You Dismay" spirit, the publicity men have paraded their ranks of beauty in a welter of synthetic snow, reindeers released from captivity in the studio carpenter's shop, and elegant wrappings for gifts that will never see the inside of a stocking. The studio snow lay round about, deep and crisp and even, when Esther Williams came in sight, taking a chance that the frost would not be too cruel, with just a touch of red satin and white fur above and below, and a winsome smile, to keep out the cold. In case you hadn't guessed she had come, in the words of Metro-Goldwyn-Mayer's caption-writer, to "portray Santa Claus in the spirit of Christmas." The reindeer, snow, and dolls helped a lot, because otherwise the costume is remarkably near the Robinson Crusoe tradition and no-one wants to think of Esther Williams mooning around alone on a desert island at this time of the year.

Esther Williams' dream of a white Christmas. Dainty beach shoes, as the fashion writers say, complete a two-piece ensemble. It was a masterpiece of forethought to include a pair of really warm, serviceable gloves.

Ava Gardner has the Christmas spirit hanging up on the door. Three-league boots for snowstorm wear are being worn with five-inch heels this season.

Ann Sheridan has a snowball scheme. Snowballs, like everything else manufactured at Hollywood, are soignée—unlike the rough, handmade finish.

15

the first British military paper, a bi-weekly. When the British occupied Beirut the *Eastern Times* ceased publication; for the seven days until the paper restarted, the British produced *Ninth Army News*. The first British newspaper in North Africa, after the Allied invasion in November 1942, was the *Tripoli Times*. The Pink Elephant Division of the British army in Persia and Iraq in 1945 had the magazine *Piac*, and among the service contributors were men of the Royal Fusiliers and the Royal Sussex Regiment.

Imperial and Commonwealth troops had their own publications.

29

Springbok, the official newspaper of the South African forces in the Middle East, was first published in Cairo on 23 October 1941, as a weekly. It was an efficiently produced twelve-page newspaper, liberally illustrated with photographs and cartoons, and contained items in English and Afrikaans. Among regular features were a centre-spread of photographs; 'Bully and Klinker', a jokes column; 'News Flashes from all the Provinces'; and cartoons by Theo Kramer. There were also reprints of articles and cartoons from South African papers such as the *Natal Daily News* and the *Rand Daily Mail*, as well as poems in English and Afrikaans. A special feature typical of the cultural side of the newspaper's comprehensive contents was a centre-spread of 4 December 1941 entitled 'War Artists on Parade', made up of photographs of paintings by South African artists such as Neville Lewis and Geoffrey Long, official war artists who visited the Libyan Desert to paint war scenes.

In 1941 a front-page announcement headlined, 'Tell them we are proud of them. From every part of South Africa, this message comes to the Springboks fighting in the Libyan Desert.' Under the caption 'Roll of Honour', *Springbok* printed long casualty lists of their fighting forces, and on 24 December 1942 there were several stories in memoriam to Maj.-Gen. Dan Pienaar, killed with eleven others in an air accident in Kenya. A tough and capable South African general who had served from the early fighting at El Wak to El Alamein, Pienaar had played a big part in halting Rommel.

On 2 May 1942, the first issue of the *Canadian Press News*, a four-page weekly published in London by P.R. Services, Canadian Military H.Q., for free distribution to 'the Canadian Forces Overseas', contained the following message from the Canadian Defence Chiefs:

> The welfare of every Canadian in the three fighting services is first and foremost in the hearts and minds of all Canadians at home. The *Canadian Press News* comes to you Canadians overseas in the hope that it will fill a longfelt need with news of Canada and what the home folks are doing and saying and thinking while you are away. It may not be quite the equivalent of your hometown newspaper: you will readily realize it couldn't be. But it will help to keep Canada fresh in your minds: it will be a link with home. We know you will appreciate it. We know, too, that you will join with us in expressing that appreciation to the Canadian Press for the voluntary service 'CP' is rendering in taking full charge of compiling and editing the paper for the Canadian Government.

On 19 August 1942, Canadians took the major part in a large-scale raid on Dieppe when they went ashore and fought the Germans for nine hours before withdrawing. Of the Dieppe raid, Lieutenant-General Stuart, Chief of the Canadian General Staff, said in the *Canadian Press News* of 29 August 1942, 'We walked into the Boche's parlor through the front door at a time we chose and left through

Basic training the Navy way; a cartoon page from the Navy issue of *Yank*.

THIS MEANS OUT OF BOUNDS

Make a good mental picture of this sign. It is a new international sign which means out-of-bounds (off limits) to all ranks of every Allied Army, in any language.

Already it is in use in the 8th Army, where troops of many different tongues are serving together. Now, owing to difficulties experienced by non-English-speaking troops, it is to be adopted throughout this theatre.

You will see it exhibited close to the written notices at the entrance to all out-of-bounds areas—on buildings, shops, bars and restaurants where entrance is forbidden to Allied troops.

Remember this sign—AND REMEMBER WHAT IT MEANS.

TO ALL TROOPS

the same door when we wanted to leave.' The general might have mentioned that out of a total of 5,000 Canadians who went through that door, nearly 3,500 never came out. They remained behind – killed, wounded, or prisoners-of-war.

On Friday, 14 January 1944, Vol. 1, No. 1, of the Italy edition of *Maple Leaf* with *Canadian Press News*, for 'Canadian Troops in Action', made its appearance. Published in Italy for the Canadian armed forces by the Canadian Army P.R. Unit, with Lieut.-Col. R. S. Malone as the editor-in-chief and Capt. J. D. Macfarlane as managing editor, it was produced with the help of the staff of *Eighth Army News* and *Stars and Stripes*. Under its banner it stated baldly, 'Contents passed by Censor.' It did not take long for the newspaper to become established as a daily.

A regular feature was a cartoon by staff artist Sgt. W. G. Coughlin, boldly drawn and barbed, reminiscent of the work of American Bill Mauldin, and extremely popular. (*This Army*, a book of Coughlin's cartoons, was published in December 1944.) Other cartoons in *Maple Leaf* included 'Burp' by Tattersall, and 'Blondie', Chic Young's famous strip cartoon. Staff personnel included writers Sgt. Howard Rutsey and Sgt. Joe Greaves and photographers Sgt. E. Kerr and Gunner E. Foote. A popular feature was 'Rhyme and Reason'. Besides articles and features specially written for *Maple Leaf* by the staff writers, others were reprinted from Allied service publications and from the non-military press, for instance those by Wallace Rayburn, war correspondent of the *Montreal Standard*.

On 7 March 1944, a front-page *Maple Leaf* news story about the first award of a Victoria Cross in Sicily-Italy to a Canadian, Maj. Paul Triquet, for courage and leadership in the battle for Casa Berardi, was illustrated with a strong line-impression by Sgt. W. G. Coughlin.

As the Allies moved into Naples, Rome, and other Italian cities, the Allied press frequently exposed the unsavoury involvement of

32

Service Copy

VICTORY

Vol. II   No. 7

★ ON THE MAIL RUN BY RICHARD BUSVINE
★ LAST TRAIN FROM FRANCE BY ALAN MOOREHEAD

4 AS.

When thighs were in fashion! This high-kicker dancing
on the camouflaged nacelle of an aircraft
amply covers the front of a service
copy of *Victory*.

Italian crack sharpshooters, the Bersaglieri, were distinguished
by the feathers attached to their helmets and the
speed with which they marched. Here they
storm a Russian bunker. *Signal*.

Allied troops in hold-ups, robberies, and various rackets such as black-market selling of food, medical supplies, and petrol. On 9 November 1944, under the headline 'Allied Police Crack Deserters', *Maple Leaf* printed a long report about gangs of deserters from units of the U.S. and Canadian forces and the Foreign Legion, and Italian and Spanish crooks, who were terrorizing Rome and Naples with their depredations and rivalries. One serious incident concerned two U.S. deserters arrested in a 'shoot out' with military police and found to be infected with V.D. They were transferred to hospital, where fellow gangsters dressed as military police made an abortive attempt to rescue them.

Incorporated in the Italy (Rome) edition of *Maple Leaf*, published by the First Echelon, C.M.F. in December 1944, was a novel free gift of a fold-and-cut version of *Reader's Digest*. Following the invasion of Normandy in June 1944, *Maple Leaf* was published in Caen for the Canadian armed forces who had captured this key city after bitter fighting.

Besides *The Crusader* and *Eighth Army News* the Australians in the Middle East had their own *A.I.F. News*. In New Guinea they had *Guinea Gold*, published in Port Moresby. There was also an American edition of *Guinea Gold* for U.S. troops serving in New Guinea. Copies of the newspaper were flown each day over the Owen Stanley Range to Buna, Gona, and down to Milne Bay. New Zealand troops in Italy had their weekly, *New Zealand Times*.

Hundreds of small units produced their own newspapers one way or another. Some were just wall newspapers or stencilled sheets, but a good deal of enthusiasm and effort went into their production. 362/139 Field Regiment R.A. produced a wall newspaper, *Avalanche*, first published in India, which journeyed from Poona through Burma to the Rangoon area. At Port Swettenham in Malaya, Lieut. J. C. Andrews, R.N.V.R., published *Brand Flash* from an old railroad shed within twenty-four hours of the naval landing in 1945. The two-page journal featured home news, local gossip, and a matrimonial and problems advice service. Sailors queued for copies every day.

Another naval news-sheet, *Barbary News*, was shown at an exhibition of service newspapers in London in 1945. One story in the *Barbary News* was about Admiral the Earl of Cork and Orrery, a legendary figure in the Navy who sported a monocle and was noted for his impressive reading of the lessons in church. One day the small daughter of a petty officer was asked if she had enjoyed the service, and replied that it was most impressive 'when God got up and spoke'. The story was told to the admiral, who commented, 'It was a very natural mistake on the part of the child.'

The Navy was the official organ of the Navy League, but a popular Navy publication was the *Pacific Post*, the daily newspaper of the British Pacific Fleet, published from August 1945 in Sydney, Australia. It was heralded as the first paper written, edited, and printed by men of the Navy for men in the Navy.

ROYAL
AIR FORCE
JOURNAL

MIDDLE EAST EDITION

Number 20   27th February, 1943

The *Royal Air Force Journal*, published fortnightly, proclaimed that its purpose was to give all ranks of the service information and news 'not usually released to the Press'. It also stated that 'Contributions, which should not be controversial, would be welcomed.' Its features included articles – humorous and serious – short stories, photographs, cartoons, and line drawings. Contributors were normally Air Force personnel and included Flt.-Lt. F. Ogilvy, Flt.-Lt. John Pudney, Sgt. A. J. Tucker, and *Punch* cartoonist David Langdon.

Soldier, the 'British Army Magazine', which today carries on the traditions of British service publications of World War II, was first produced as a fortnightly by the War Office (AWS 3) and 21 Army Group (Welfare Service) and printed for H.Q. 21 Army Group in Brussels early in 1945. Run by No. 1 British Army Newspaper Unit, B.L.A., the twenty-four-page magazine was similar in format to *Picture Post* but carried many more pictures. Its contents included a variety of articles, pin-ups, photographic features, cartoons, chess, crosswords and quizzes and 'To Soldier', a regular page for brief letters from readers. Advertisements were not accepted. After the surrender of Germany the magazine was published in Hamburg for sale to members of the British and Allied forces in B.L.A.

Blighty, a magazine published in London from late 1940, on sale to the public and issued free to the forces abroad, was officially distributed by the Admiralty, the War Office, the Air Ministry, and the British and Indian Red Cross, but was not produced by the forces. The magazine was chiefly made up of joke cartoons and short stories by civilians, although two pages were devoted to poems and cartoons submitted by servicemen, who were awarded small prizes for their trouble. Firms taking nominal squares of advertising space contributed to the distribution costs. Patrons of *Blighty* included Clement Attlee, Winston Churchill, the Earl of Derby, Lord Newall, and Lord Nuffield.

3D 3D

THE STARS AND STRIPES

Weekly Newspaper of the U.S. Armed Forces in the British Isles

Vol. 2 No. 2 | London, England | April 25, 1942

General Marshall Inspects Troops in Northern Ireland

Gen. George C. Marshall, Chief of Staff of the Army, watches an Infantry unit march in review during his visit last weekend to Northern Ireland and the American troops stationed there. With General Marshall as he visited the troops were a number of high ranking Army officers and other officials of the British, Northern Ireland and United States governments. The officers included . . .

. . . Maj. Gen. R. P. Hartle, commander of U.S. troops in Northern Ireland, Lt. Gen. H. E. Franklyn, commander of British troops in Northern Ireland, and Maj. Gen. James E. Chaney, commander of American troops in the British Isles. General Hartle stands next to General Marshall, while General Chaney is at right. Story Page 3. (Associated Press Photos.)

Tell Pass Plan, Trips to London

Leaves and furloughs for a limited number of American troops in Northern Ireland will be granted after May 1, Maj. Gen. James E. Chaney, commander of United States Army Forces in the British Isles, announced Friday.

Nine days will be the maximum time for which either leaves or furloughs may be granted, but those having passes will be permitted to visit England, Scotland or Wales.

Of the total number allowed to be absent from their duties, no more than 50 men and 10 officers will be given permission to visit London, the remainder of those excused from duty being obliged to spend their holiday in other parts of the country.

Individuals may not have more than one leave or furlough in any three-month period and not more than 7 per cent. of a command may be absent at one time.

* * *

Men going on leave or furlough must:

1. Have sufficient funds to cover all traveling expenses during their trip and must purchase return-trip tickets before departure.
2. Have a furlough certificate or leave order.
3. Have their identity card.
4. Have British embarkation forms.
5. Have British leave ration book.
6. Have identification tags.
7. Have gas mask and helmet.

Other equipment will not be carried and hand luggage should be limited to what the individual can carry and maintain supervision over.

The route selected for travel of troops to and from Northern Ireland is such that meals may be obtained en route and personnel, therefore, need not carry luncheons when leaving their home stations.

* * *

Arrangements have been completed whereby men on leave or furlough who may become ill will be treated at the nearest British Army, Naval or R.A.F. station and at the Railway Transportation Offices in various railroad stations. Personnel becoming ill in London may visit a special Army dispensary which has been set up.

The American Red Cross field director will make arrangements for men wishing to avail themselves of invitations to visit private homes.

Pay Boosts Near Vote

WASHINGTON, D.C. (Special Cable from Associated Press)—Bills to raise the pay of soldiers, sailors and marines, Friday were approaching final action in Congress.

The Johnson bill, providing for an increase from $21 a month to $42 a month for privates and for corresponding increases through all grades and ranks to include second lieutenants, already has been passed by the Senate and now is being studied by a special military affairs subcommittee of the House.

At the same time, the War Department is sponsoring another measure which would provide subsistence allowances for all men in the services. This bill also would grant additional funds to dependents of service men whose allowances are insufficient to meet living expenses.

Several other measures of interest to the Armed Forces also are pending, including one which would defer income tax obligations until six months after termination of service.

Dear Mom: I've Met 2 Heroes

SOMEWHERE IN NORTHERN IRELAND—Dear Mom: Let's forget about the sights I'm seeing and the things I'm doing this time, Mom. I want to tell you about some of the things I've been thinking since I first landed in Northern Ireland.

I guess maybe it's because I've been a little ashamed of myself and telling you about it will make me feel better.

You see, Mom, Americans, and especially American soldiers, are a queer breed. We like to think we're rough and tough, and we like to "take over."

I remember reading somewhere that America is a nation with a thousand mothers and a thousand fathers. Maybe that's the reason we want every one to think we're the original "Dead End Kids."

But too often, Mom, we get the idea that we've got a monopoly on the world's supply of courage. I suppose we have our share. You can tell a Yankee soldier anywhere. If he came into a store dressed in only a sheet you could spot him for a Yankee by the air of confidence he wears like a coat, by the look in his eye. You seldom see a Yankee not perfectly at ease, no matter what the surroundings.

T-Bone Steak

But here's what I mean. At first we got a big kick out of going into a restaurant and asking for a big T-bone steak, with fresh green beans, celery, mashed potatoes, apple pie and all the trimmings.

We knew darn well the chances were pretty good we wouldn't get it, but we wanted every one to know that's what we were used to before.

Well, Mom, we don't do things like that now. And we don't go into dime stores and ask for three bars of soap. And we don't ask anyone where we can get "some good American cigarettes." Nobody told us to stop doing those nasty little things. We just came around to it gradually.

And it's because, whatever and Heroes - - - -

(Continued on Page 5)

Kansas City Police Sniff Breaths for Traces of Liquor

KANSAS CITY, MO. (Special Cable from Associated Press)—Kansas City police are halting city-bound cars Friday and Saturday nights and sniffing drivers' breaths to determine whether they have been drinking.

Police assigned to sniff must prove they haven't head colds, which would impair their smelling.

3 Weeks Holds Burma's Fate

CHUNGKING, CHINA — The next three weeks may seal Burma's fate.

They will decide whether the Japanese can reach the high and dry ground of the upper valleys in the race against the monsoons due by May 14.

They will reveal Japan's capacity to maintain her already over-taxed supply lines during the rainy season and to keep up the pressure necessary to expel the Allies.

Radio Program

The first of a series of radio programs for American troops will be broadcast Monday from 8.30 to 7.30 p.m. by the British Broadcasting Corporation. The program, arranged by the War Department, will feature guest stars.

News from American shortwave stations may be picked up at 6 p.m., while a number of commercial programs now are being sent via shortwave from the United States.

U.S. Rations Gasoline in 17 East States

WASHINGTON, D.C. (UP)—A temporary gasoline rationing plan is to be put into operation in 17 East Coast states May 15. The ration is expected to allow each motorist between two and a half and five gallons per week.

Boys Will Be Boys

WASHINGTON, D.C. (UP)—Japanese diplomats interned at Hot Springs, Va., have discarded western dress for the kimono—and a fan.

Tokyo Raid Upsets Japs

* * *

See U.S. Blows at Nazis

— Tokyo —
By Drew Middleton
(Associated Press Staff Correspondent)

American bombers, flying high, wide and handsome over the supposedly sacred islands of Japan, hammered Tokyo, Kobe, Yokohama and four other cities last Saturday as the United States began sure repayment for Pearl Harbor.

By Japanese accounts only schools, hospitals and "cultural establishments" were hit. But the Japs have admitted damage by fire and there is no doubt that the bombers battered the heavy industries centered around Kobe and Yokohama.

This bold raid, which hit the body of the Japanese octopus as its tentacles felt southwards toward Australia and westward toward India, was the climax of a week of stirring Allied air successes.

It followed closely Brigadier General Royce's dashing attack on the Japanese in the Philippines from Australia and occurred almost simultaneously with the Royal Air Force's gallant and damaging blow at the great German factory at Augsburg.

Damage

The United Nations still await details of the raid on Japan. Thus far there has been no official word from Washington. The Associated Press has heard unvarying praise of the raid here in London. Most British officers believe considerable damage was done.

* * * *

There are good reasons for an official silence in Washington.

If the raid was made by planes from an aircraft carrier, the ship must maintain radio silence until she is out of the cruising radius of Japanese submarines and patrol bombers.

Moreover, it is obvious the Japanese have no idea where the raiders came from or what was their destination. The Japanese high command, therefore, cannot make tactical dispositions to meet Tokyo - - -

(Continued on Page 3)

— Nazis —
By Edward W. Beattie
(United Press Staff Correspondent)

As spring wears on toward the halfway mark and the usual spring hatch of rumors reaches a late April peak, Britain and Germany are dug in on two sides of their narrow sea—each prepared to defend itself against invasion.

As is usual during periods when the chief problem is "What that man is going to do next," the chief focus is on Adolf Hitler, although Nazi Field Marshal Karl Rudolf Gerd von Rundstedt and Sir Alan Brooke, British commander, may be pardoned for their considerable interest in each others specific plans for the months before the weather breaks sometime in late September.

Rundstedt, who is Hitler's commander in western Europe, probably would like to know, too, what Sir Alan and Gen. George C. Marshall, United States Chief of Staff, talked about because, according to all indications, German defenses along the great occupied coastline are going to have a very busy summer.

* * *

The coastline on both sides of the Channel can be penetrated by Commando raids and pounded with bombers during the next several months—but invading either with heavy forces and making the invasion stick is a problem which must be measured in scores of divisions, and thousands of guns and tanks, not to mention ships to transport the troops and then keep supplies rolling to them.

There has been unmistakable evidence recently, however, that the Germans are worried seriously by the growing aggressive spirit on this side of the Channel.

They know it will not be long before United States bombers begin to join the Royal Air Force in battering Germany and they know, too, that many thousands of United States troops soon will be perched in the British Isles, ready to jump upon any weak point in the Nazi defenses.

In Norway, where the normal War - - -

(Continued on Page 3)

Stars and
Stripes Forever

In September 1940, the Congress of the United States passed the Selective Training and Service Act, the first conscription law ever enacted while America was at peace, providing for the annual induction of 900,000 men. In November the first group of conscripts were called up, and on 11 December 1941, four days after the United States entered the war, the scope of the act was broadened to allow for the rapid expansion of the armed forces.

Drawings from *Cavalry Journal*, U.S.A. (*and overleaf*).

Tell them what you'd like to learn and where
they're apt to find it,
Or all they'll get is a ball marked eight and
you'll be right behind it!

The hundreds of thousands of civilians inducted into various branches of the services to undergo basic and specialist training found themselves posted to camps all over America, often thousands of miles from home. Wherever they were stationed they could read the local papers and the familiar national magazines, so the rookies were not short of reading matter. Moreover many branches of the U.S. services at various levels, as well as camps and specialist units, already had their own publications, and additional publications were inaugurated to cater for newly created service establishments and newly formed units. Artists, writers, journalists, and cartoonists drafted into the services were often called upon to contribute to service publications such as *Cavalry Journal*, the Ordnance magazine, *Army Motors*, *45th Division Magazine*, *Air Force Magazine*, and the *Bureau of Naval Personnel Magazine*. Some artists and writers were employed by Camp Newspaper Services which provided features and clip-sheets for service publications. Before the end of the war the importance

'... Mom: I've met 2 Heroes.'
The *Stars and Stripes* for Americans overseas.

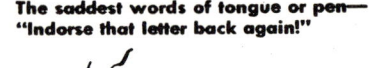

The saddest words of tongue or pen—
"Indorse that letter back again!"

Don't cause a great preponderance
Of needless correspondence!

and scope of service publications, and the circulation of the many editions of comprehensive army papers such as *Yank* and *Stars and Stripes*, had grown to such an extent that hundreds of service personnel were employed in their production on a regular or freelance basis.

CWO Will Eisner was well known for 'Joe Dope', a feature he drew for *Army Motors*. Cartoonist Mort Leav, drafted into the army in 1943, became an illustrator for army magazines and is remembered for his caricatures of Hitler as a hairy, unkempt, petty tyrant. New Yorker Bernard Kassoy, formerly a teacher of fine arts and a brilliant painter and international exhibitor, whose painting in oils 'We won the war . . .' received wide acclaim in Europe as well as in America, worked on camp newspapers in the United States early in the war. While serving as a sergeant in South-East Asia in 1944 and 1945, he contrived to paint, often under brutal conditions, and contributed serious commentaries on various aspects of art to American and British service publications.

Internationally famous cartoonist Milton Caniff, creator of the pre-war strips 'Terry and the Pirates' and 'Steve Canyon', was drawing a strip for the American troops in Burma until the Chicago Herald-Tribune Syndicate objected to the use of their character. In 1943, Caniff created 'Male Call' for the Camp Newspaper Services, for distribution to service publications. Caniff accepted no fee for his services. Another Camp Services feature was the 'Wolf' by Sgt. Leonard Sansone.

Superfluous papers
Make arduous labors.

Drawing from *Air Force Magazine*, U.S.A.

In 1940, the *Daily Oklahoman*, then owned by the colonel publisher of the *45th Division News*, provided and paid for material used by the service newspaper. Bill Mauldin, while still an army trainee, began his cartoon career with a series of panel cartoons in the civilian newspaper the *Daily Oklahoman*, about the pitfalls and grinding routine of army life. This was reprinted in the *45th Division News*. Mauldin's first panel for his divisional newspaper featured two draftees who became famous as Willie and Joe of 'Up Front'.

The 'Joe Dope' strip cartoon by C.W.O. Will Eisner from Ordnance magazine *Army Motors*.

In 1941, Mauldin's first cartoon book, *Star Spangled Banter*, was published, featuring these characters. He continued his work with the *45th Division News* and the *Daily Oklahoman* until early 1943, as well as submitting other panels and gags to *Yank*.

Following the invasion of Sicily in July 1943, Mauldin's work continued to appear in the *45th Division News*, which was the first U.S. army newspaper to be published on European soil in World War II. In the summer of 1943 a second Mauldin collection, *Sicily Sketchbook*, was printed in Palermo, Sicily, for G.I. sales. By Christmas, with Mauldin stationed in Naples, his *45th Division News* cartoon was appearing in the official army newspaper, *Stars and Stripes*, and his third collection of cartoons, *Mud, Mules and Mountains*, was published. Mauldin was transferred to the staff of *Stars and Stripes*, and his final European collection, *This Damn Tree Leaks*, was published by *Stars and Stripes* in Italy in 1945.

Cartoonist Bill Mauldin of
Stars and Stripes in Italy, 1944.

Within a few months of Pearl Harbor and the precipitation of America into the war, it was decided to publish an official entertainment and historical magazine for the American army, to be called *Yank*. A strip cartoon drawn by David Breger for King Features Syndicate, appearing in the *Saturday Evening Post* on 30 August 1941, was taken up by publications all over the United States and caught the attention of the *Yank* magazine men, who thought Breger's work, with its acid views and individual wit, ideal for inclusion in their proposed format. Since the new publication was to be entirely filled with work executed specially for the magazine by enlisted men, however, the syndicated strip called 'Private Breger' could not be

Two panel cartoons by Bill Mauldin from *Stars and Stripes*.

"WHY THE HELL COULDN'T YOU HAVE BEEN BORN A BEAUTIFUL WOMAN?"

"NONSENSE. G-2(I) REPORTED THAT MACHINE GUN SILENCED HOURS AGO. STOP WIGGLING YOUR FINGERS AT ME"

used. Breger therefore agreed to draw a separate weekly panel with a new title for *Yank*, and came up with the name 'G.I. Joe' (from 'Government Issue'). The *Yank* people were delighted with the idea and the strip appeared in the first issue of *Yank* on 17 June 1942. The name 'G.I. Joe' captured the imagination of the general public and service personnel alike, and within a week of the appearance of *Yank*, the term was being used throughout the services and soon after that it spread all over the United States. It had become the appellation for the American soldier of World War II as 'doughboy' or 'Yank' had symbolized the ordinary American soldier of World War I.

The Sad Sack

Two 'Sad Sack' cartoons by George Baker from *Yank*.

41

The first permanent feature selected in spring 1942 for the as yet unpublished *Yank* magazine had been the work of George Baker (1915–1975), who had worked for four years as an animator and striker for Disney. He joined the army in June 1941, and a year later his creation 'Sad Sack' appeared in *Yank*. Based on an army term for a useless soldier, 'a sad sack of shit', 'Sad Sack' was, according to Baker, 'an average soldier steeped in psychological if not actual reality' and reflected the soldier's state of mind, resigned, tired, helpless, beaten. A variant of the classic 'little man', another 'Good Soldier Schweik', he was one of the most popular cartoon characters to come out of the war, even surpassing the popularity of G.I. Joe, and in over three and a half years with *Yank*, Sad Sack saw service in every theatre of war and on every front. Sack's many tormentors were usually loud-mouthed master sergeants. The world seemed to conspire against him and trouble was his natural element. He never got the girl, regulations defied his sincerest efforts, and everyone took advantage of him. In Sack, *Yank* found the ideal soldier character, reflecting the frustrations and bugbears of service life and at the same time supplying a scapegoat, someone even a real-life Sack could

" So yer in the Home Guard are yer Buddy ? Hum . . . Say I didn't
know things was as bad as that."

look down on and laugh at, and so find consolation in somebody
else's torment.

Besides cartoons, photos, and short feature articles, *Yank* also
published readers' poems and letters. By the end of the war, *Yank*
had developed into a large organization, and editions with the motto
'By the men . . . for the men in the service' were produced all over
the world from Britain to Australia and the Pacific. The British edition
was first published on 8 November 1942. The main editorial office
was in New York, but offices were maintained in Washington, France,
Italy, Australia-Philippines, the Central Pacific, the Marianas, Burma-
India and China, Alaska, Iran, Panama, Brazil, Bermuda, Iceland,

43

the Middle East, and Newfoundland. A separate editorial staff was established for a Navy edition.

Managing editors, editors, and the hundreds of editorial and production staff were all enlisted men with ranks no higher than sergeant or the equivalent naval rank, but Bureau officers were in charge of all editorial offices and the magazine's contents were censored by the U.S. military censors. Editorial staff included Sgt. Joe McCarthy, Sgt. Durbin L. Horner, Sgt. Merle Miller, and Pfc John O. Armstrong, editors; Sgt. Arthur Weithaus, Sgt. Frank Brandt, and Sgt. Ralph Stein, art directors; and Cpl. Margaret Davis, associate editor, one of the few women employed on the *Yank* editorial staff.

Vol. III No. 31.   Delhi, Thursday, April 12, 1945.   Reg. No. L5015

Masthead from the authoritative American service newspaper *Roundup*.

Stars and Stripes was published in several editions, first as a weekly newspaper for the U.S. armed forces, and later as a daily in the Mediterranean and Italy with a weekly magazine supplement. The British edition was published soon after the first American troops arrived in Northern Ireland in February 1942. One of the early cartoon features in *Stars and Stripes* was drawn by Bruce Bairnsfather, the most famous cartoonist of World War I and creator of 'Old Bill', who now turned up in the Home Guard. Another *Stars and Stripes* cartoonist who achieved a wide reputation was Sgt. Dick Wingert.

On 8 November 1942, Allied forces landed on the French North African coast and on 11 November Allied Forces H.Q., North Africa, reported that the French commander, Admiral Darlan, had ordered a cease-fire in the whole of Algeria and Morocco. A month later, with the Allies massing in the Tebourba area, twenty miles west of Tunis, and Allied planes raiding from Bizerta in Tunisia all the way to Marble Arch in Libya, *Stars and Stripes* made its first appearance in North Africa on 10 December 1942 as a four-page weekly. It was produced with the collaboration of the staff of *Yank* and printed at the office of the *Eczo Algiers* by U.S. printers working with Frenchmen on rundown machines and using fonts of type which had no dollar signs, *w*'s, or *k*'s. General Eisenhower sent a message to the first issue stressing the importance of the editorial function in war and of home news to the soldiers.

Another all-American service newspaper was *Roundup*, 'By the Men for the Men'. Published in New Delhi, India, first for the China-India-Burma theatre and later for the India-Burma theatre, it was widely read by American and British servicemen. Articles from *Roundup* were often reprinted in British and Australian service publications as well as other U.S. publications. Such an article was one reprinted in the Middle East edition of *Royal Air Force Journal* on 27 February 1943. Said to be one of the most dramatic stories of the war, it was told in the actual words of Corporal Campanella of the U.S.A.F., who, with Lieut. Cecil Williams, was lost in the jungles of north-west Burma for twenty-three days after baling out of a transport aircraft.

As with other American service papers, most of *Roundup*'s staff and contributors were enlisted personnel. In 1944 and 1945 they included Capt. Floyd 'Bucky' Walter, editor, and his acting editor, Lieut. Boyd Sinclair, who often wrote the editorials 'The War Warmed Over'; and a sergeant, Charles W. Clark, who wrote a column called 'Briefs from the Brambles'. Staff writers included Staff Sgt. Karl Peterson, T/Sgt. Arthur Heenan, and someone whose by-line was T/7 Osmosis Fink. Field correspondents included a Pfc, John Randolph, and a sergeant, Alan Kayes. Contributions were supplied by other editorial personnel, and news items came from soldier correspondents, the United Press, OWI, and Army News Services. The circulation manager of *Roundup* was a lieutenant, S. R. Rose.

Roundup often featured two full pages of sports news, local and from home and abroad, covering football, baseball, basketball, boxing, hockey, and golf as well as news and gossip of sportsmen serving in the forces. Typical were these headlines in the issue of 1 March 1945: 'Navy Tumbles: Iowa Grabs Big Ten Lead', 'American Golfers Down British 8–7', 'Tommy Gomez, Pug, Wounded by Nazis', 'Evacs Capture Burma Basketball Honors', and 'Robinson withstands Hectic Sixth to Beat Lamotta'.

An unusual service publication for all Allied personnel serving in South-East Asia was *Phoenix*, which made its debut on 24 February 1945. Named for the insignia of the Allied troops there, it was a weekly picture magazine published by the South-East Asia Command under a joint British-American editorial staff.

In general appearance *Phoenix* resembled *Life*, having a similar format. Editorial content consisted for the most part of pictures covering the local scene and troop activities, and news pictures from the Home Front. Writer-cameramen, both British and American, covered the fighting areas, moving forward with the advancing troops and also reporting from forward airfields. Regular features included an exclusive Washington letter, American sports pictures, and pictorial news features.

Originally conceived by Gen. Joseph W. Stilwell and Lord Louis Mountbatten, the magazine was months in preparation. The co-editors were Capt. Ian Coster, R.M., from *Seac*, and Capt. Crosby Maynard, U.S.A.F., a former associate editor of *Roundup*.

45

The Army News Service (ANS) supplied material to the editorial offices of service papers in every theatre of war. Special staff features, photos, and articles from various service newspapers were reprinted by other service newspapers, often without accrediting the original source, and articles and cartoons from non-service newspapers and magazines were also reprinted from time to time. Servicemen in all parts of the world were thus able to form some idea of what their counterparts in other theatres were doing. News services in the United States and other parts of the world supplied material from the Home Front and foreign news.

In April 1945 an ANS item sent out from New Orleans told the story of a thirty-six-year-old former soldier, Hugh Callan, remanded to Atlanta to begin a twenty-year federal sentence imposed by a Camp Blanding, Fla., court martial for making uncomplimentary remarks about President Roosevelt. It was stated that Callan intended to carry his fight to the Supreme Court to seek vindication. The report was published in several service newspapers without comment.

Sent out from Philadelphia at about the same time was another ANS item which reported that Dr J. P. Skelton of the University of Pennsylvania had stated that week that if Junior was delinquent maybe Dad was beefing too much about Roosevelt and the Administration and that 'continual cursing of Roosevelt and criticism of the Administration is part of the influence these youngsters are absorbing'. According to Dr Skelton such anti-authority attitudes were not lost on juvenile delinquents.

Yet another story released at the same time from the United Press in Washington was reprinted in several service newspapers. It concerned Congressman William J. Callagher, a former street sweeper who had given up his Minneapolis pension to go to Congress. In his maiden speech he warned Republicans that if they did not stop 'singing songs of hate against the President they, like the Whigs, would pass out of the picture in less than four years'.

From Washington in March 1945 came an ANS and UP story taken up by service newspapers, about a fight between two Democratic congressmen, John Rankin of Mississipi and Frank E. Hook of Michigan. It was reported that Rankin had called Hook a Communist and Hook called Rankin a 'goddamn liar'. Following the name-calling the two men made a rush for each other and began a pummelling and wrestling match until astounded congressmen forcibly separated them.

Sometimes items slipped into the service papers which were salutary reminders to the G.I.s that there was 'no percentage in trying to buck the system'. Early in 1945 a Press Association photo appeared in service papers of a private, formerly a shipyard worker, sentenced to hang by an army court martial for refusal to drill. Later his sentence was commuted to life imprisonment and then to five years hard labour.

In March 1945 from the Pacific came an ANS report with a bitter taste. The Hood River branch of the American Legion had recently

The world's history of entertainment captured in this full-page advertisement from *Ceylon Review*, 1945.

struck the names of sixteen soldiers off the county memorial lists because they were of Japanese-American parentage, and following nationwide criticism the Legion had offered to restore their names if they could prove they were loyal to the United States and not to Hirohito. The report continued that the Legion could put the name of twenty-five-year-old Frank T. Hachi of Portland, Oregon, back on the list as the Army had stated that he had died as the result of a dangerous volunteer mission on Leyte. Most of the men in his regiment had volunteered to give blood to save his life. The sterling qualities and brave service of Nisei troops in Europe and the Pacific were usually given fair coverage in all service papers.

An amusing note was struck by an ANS report from London in February 1944 which appeared in *Roundup* under the cynical headline 'Fu Manchu Dies For His Country'. According to the report, Sax Rohmer, who had been thrilling readers of mysteries with the doings of the 'insidious' Dr Fu Manchu for years, had announced that Fu had died a literary death for his country. Rohmer said that the Chinese government of Chiang Kai-shek had 'simply raised hell' about his Fu character, insisting that it 'was influencing world opinion of the Chinese and that it was astonishing bad propaganda for an ally to be putting out'. The author had appealed to Wellington Koo, the Chinese ambassador to Britain, but without avail.

Strip cartoon from *Yank*.

Another ANS item, sent out at the end of 1944, that amused the bewhiskered veterans sweating it out in the campaign areas of Europe, South-East Asia, and the Pacific, came from Lewiston, Ohio. Forty-four-year-old William C. Morland, who had taken to the hills when Roosevelt was elected President in 1932, and had stayed there ever since, was in jail charged with draft evasion and stealing from forest rangers whom he had led on a 'merry chase' before they finally trapped him. Morland said, 'I went into the hills when Roosevelt beat Hoover and the Federals have been after me ever since for borrowing clothes and stuff from the ranger stations.' Surprised to hear there was a war on, he had asked, 'Who got us into that?'

Service Copy

VICTORY

Vol. II   No. 9

★ I LOVE ENGLAND BY JAMES HILTON
★ BURMA BATTLE
★ MEET SAPPER STONE

4 AS.

A wide variety of battle features and patriotic articles entertained
and informed the troops, and enlivened hours
of boredom on the way to victory.

The Wehrmacht in action. German troops manhandle a gun into
position in France. This illustration is from the
popular German magazine *Signal*, which
became a vital morale-booster for the
Wehrmacht and its allies.

He said that he had eluded rangers by walking backwards in snow-shoes or using an extra pair on poles to leave reversed tracks.

Less amusing was a report from ANS reprinted in several service newspapers as the Allies invaded Germany. Men of the Seventh Army were said to have been battling women and girls who had attacked American infantry and armoured vehicles with grenades and bazookas on the east bank of the river Main. The report stated that scores of women had sniped from hiding places at the 45th Division as it crossed the river to exploit the bridgehead, while sixteen-year-old girls had been found dropping grenades from the upper floors of houses. One fifteen-year-old had been stopped while trying to fire a bazooka at passing American tanks.

Selected articles, excerpts, cartoons, and short stories from non-service publications such as the *Saturday Evening Post* and the *New Yorker* were reprinted in both British and American service publications. Features and stories by Damon Runyon, William Saroyan, and C. S. Forrester and cartoons by Soglow, Arno, and Thurber were popular with service readers everywhere. A special edition of the *New Yorker*, miniaturized but complete, and printed on lightweight paper, was sent to American servicemen all over the world.

One British service magazine, *Ceylon Review*, read by thousands of Americans as well as Britons, often reprinted serious articles from U.S. non-service newspapers and periodicals. An article from the *New York Herald Tribune* by Walter Duranty, an authority on Russia, which was reprinted in its entirety in *Ceylon Review* in November 1944, discussed two questions: Was the Russian Revolution over, or at least was it settling down, as other revolutionary movements had done, to something more mellow and conservative? And if so what did this mean for the future of Russia, and her relations with the rest of the world? The article concluded: 'If it is now established – as I have tried to establish by a résumé of Russian development during the last twenty years – that Russia no longer wishes to impress its ideas upon other nations against their will and has indeed modified many of its earlier ideas, then it surely follows that future relations between Russia and the Western World can be peaceful and mutually advantageous.'

Service publications printed many warnings about the makeup of the German people and the consequences of their traditions, ideas, training, and upbringing, as well as arguments about the reactionary forces which had helped to create Hitler. Several writers in 1944 and 1945 made the point that for a hundred years not one class or group in Germany had been immune to Germanomania. It was reiterated that there was not one fact in the recent past to suggest a change of attitude. Early in 1945, extracts from Leopold Schwartzchild's article in the *New York Times* magazine appeared in service publications. He stated categorically that those who said the ordinary German had been led astray by a Nazi minority ignored the lessons of history, and declared that he did not believe that 'the warm rain of democracy falling on German soil, would make sprout there the buds of pacificism'.

During the American conquest of Saipan in the Marianas (14 June–8 July 1944) the Allies came into contact with Japanese civilians for the first time in the war, and this was a test and a revelation for both sides. Of course, details of the confrontation were of absorbing interest to servicemen everywhere, particularly to those moving up for what was anticipated to be the bloodiest battle in history – the fighting against fanatical Japanese on their home ground. Extracts from an article about the American occupation of Saipan and the first meeting between American soldiers and Japanese civilians, by William McGaffin in the *Saturday Evening Post* towards the end of 1944, were published in Allied service newspapers all over the world.

Servicemen often found themselves serving alongside troops of various nationalities with whom they had never before had contact, and in lands where the natives were completely alien. The British had strong traditions of service in all parts of the world with troops from all parts of the Empire, but for most Americans overseas service and foreign troops were novelties. The G.I. found himself involved with Gurkhas, Punjabis, and Jats in India, with Nagas, Kachins, and Karens in Burma, with Papuans, Solomon Islanders, and Fijians in the Pacific, and with hosts of other races serving with the Allied forces in Africa and Europe. Service publications often published vignettes, cameos, stories, and news items about these races for the benefit of service personnel in an effort to promote goodwill and understanding.

Such an article was one written by Robert Lewis Taylor, serving with the U.S. navy, about Fijian troops on Bougainville. Taylor had visited Fiji several times before the war, and gave a general impression of Fiji and the Fijians. He then went on to describe his experiences on Bougainville with Fijian scouts who, he said, 'understood the tangled greenery that covers the South Pacific islands the way a New Yorker understands Times Square'. Taylor declared that he was very impressed with the fighting qualities of the Fijians. In service publications these qualities, and many more, were usually attributed to every race serving the Allied cause.

In the *New York Times* magazine appeared an article by W. H. Laurence about Russian soldiers finding themselves chasing the Germans through 'capitalist countries' where goods and comforts long denied them were displayed. Laurence claimed that *Pravda*'s Leonid Sololeff, reporting from Bucharest, the Rumanian capital, had said that Red Army men, who had never before seen open-heeled shoes for women, fashionable for some years in capitalist countries, had advanced alternative explanations for them: either there was a shortage of leather or the Rumanians were so used to showing their heels in retreat that even the women had taken up the habit. This unlikely tale, taken up by service newspapers, was, no doubt, for amusement only,

BRITISH EDITION

YANK
THE ARMY WEEKLY

3d MAR.14
1943
VOL. 1, NO. 39

By the men .. for the men in the service

Our Readers Are Varied and Many: A Few Intellects of New Guinea

A *Yank* is something of a novelty to these New Guinean readers.

but not so was an article in *Stars and Stripes*, Italy, by Harry L. Hopkins, President Roosevelt's personal envoy, then visiting Europe, where he met important people of every description, including the Pope.

Harry ardently advocated a year's military service for all American boys of eighteen in peacetime 'as a mighty force for peace'. Servicemen read the article with mixed feelings. Here was Harry, with the war not yet over, saying, 'Our country is the one that marauders most want to conquer. What a nation to loot! What do they care if they lose two wars, or three or four if eventually they win? The final conquest of North America would make a dozen defeats worthwhile to the pillagers, and if we ever again are so weak that they have the chance to defeat us, World War Three will loom on the horizon.' This article was reprinted in several papers.

Harry L. Hopkins was not alone in expressing such opinions. P. Allen, writing in *Ceylon Review* in October 1944, stated, 'If I were a German I would not be downhearted over the way things are going. I would argue that while we could not have hoped to achieve world conquest at first effort we have been so close to it at the second that success at the third will be assured.'

Humorous articles, impressions, and nostalgic reminiscences by other ranks were always popular with readers of service newspapers and magazines, the vast majority of whom were other ranks themselves. An American G.I. in France, who before the war had worked in Paris as a musician, revisited Paris soon after the liberation and wrote an article for *Yank* about Montmartre. He had gone to the Café Pigalle, a rendezvous for musicians, and had met old friends including a Rumanian violinist with whom he had played in the summer of 1926 in the orchestra of *Blackbirds*, an all-Negro revue. This article was the type that appealed to U.S. servicemen, and it was reprinted in service papers in South-East Asia and the Pacific.

An incident reported from Paris in September 1944 and appearing in *Stars and Stripes* was a reminder that the press was always subject to military censorship and red tape. SHAEF issued a statement on 1 September 1944 to the effect that six British and American newspaper and radio correspondents had been suspended from duty by the authorities in Paris and returned to London for an inquiry for having violated the regulations in Paris on the evening of 25 August by 'putting voice broadcasts on the air over Radio Nationale'.

Stars and Stripes is still going strong today, though now it bears the strange device 'Authorized Unofficial Publication for the U.S. Armed Forces'.

The Pen is Mightier

The Sergeant got mail from his mother;
The Corporal got word from his son;
The Private was wrote by his brother;
I don't get no letters from none.

'Lament' by Yankhi, *Seac*, 1945

AMONG those millions of servicemen who were not able to express themselves by writing poems or drawing cartoons, there were thousands who were articulate enough when it came to writing letters – and many of them wielded a mighty pen. Hundreds of letters were written by servicemen to their papers, airing not only the views and sentiments of the writers but also those of their comrades. Readers' letters were on every subject. Complaints, grouses, searching questions and answers, political views and comments, and even controversial matters relating to the services, were given space in a good many papers. This did not always please the authorities. Letter writers and editorial staff sometimes found themselves in trouble with the Establishment; but able leaders such as Lord Louis Mountbatten would brook no petty interference with their newspapers.

Readers' letters – humorous, pungent, informative, and at times bitter – were as valuable to the morale of servicemen as were news, cartoons, poems, and other features. Perhaps even more so. Some of the letter writers deserved medals; some a wooden spoon, the raspberry, or a slow handclap. Not all was sweetness and light, by any means. Service rivalries, petty jealousies, bigotry, snobbery, selfishness, and class and racial discrimination were often highlighted in servicemen's letters. By and large, however, the newspapers saw to it that the correspondence published was fairly balanced. Any particularly unpalatable item in the service press, whether in the body of a publication or in the letter columns, usually got its scathing reply, one way or another. Sometimes a lively debate developed which pleased the readers. Letters usually reflected the attitudes of the services, the units and the ranks, as well as those of the publication itself.

53

In 17 December 1943 a letter to the editor from the celebrated *News Chronicle* war correspondent William Forrest, then in Italy, was published in *Union Jack*. Forrest criticized the editor for having made a scathing attack on dockers striking in Britain and for having at the same time defended his right to express opinion in wartime:

> He denies dockers the right to strike in war-time. The journalist who writes freely is doing his duty. The docker who strikes is a shirker. We shall hear the voice of the fighting men when having won the war against fascism, they go back home and return to the docks, factories, mines, farms and offices. And I shall be very surprised indeed if, when that time comes, their voice is raised against their fellow workers, for having defended the rights of labour at home, while they were away at war.

'They Write to *Seac*.' South-East Asia, 1943.

Letter columns such as 'In the Bag' in *Ceylon Review*, 'Fighting Man's Platform' in *Union Jack*, 'Mail Call' in *Yank*, 'Readers' Forum' in *Parade*, 'They Write to *Seac*', and 'F.P.O.' in *Maple Leaf*, always provided readers with food for thought, filled them with spluttering indignation, raised their spirits, or gave them a laugh or a feeling of satisfaction. Sometimes a writer provoked amusing answers to his letter, as when W. J. Reade sent *Seac* a rhyme entitled 'Hot Spot':

> One sometimes wonders, (does one not?)
> Why India is so very hot
> When other places that one knows
> Will chill the blood and freeze the toes.
> Why is it that the Indian sun,
> Which leaves our own land underdone,
> Should so immoderately roast
> And boil and bake, and sometimes toast?
> One does not know, one cannot tell,

And (tho' it rhymes so very well)
One cannot even name the spot
Which may have made this place so hot.
(One sometimes wonders, does one not?)

'Cold Snap-back!' was the reply by 'Hot Bottle':

Oh! wond'ring Reade,
I make so bold
To tell you India's very cold!
In shorts and shirts
(With rolled up sleeves),
I've shivered in a swirl of leaves!
In icy blasts
From Safed Kôh
My teeth have snapped; I'd have you know!
In places they
Don't see the sun!
(They've just had snow in Dehra Dun!)
The cold of Delhi
Seldom fails
To make the Great Ones blow their nails
No! No! Dear Sir!
I must declare
Your wond'ring leads not anywhere.

Other times readers' replies to letters in the service press were acrimonious, sarcastic, and hard hitting. Pte. E. Geldberg, in a letter to *Union Jack* at election time, 11 August 1944, did not pull his punches in lambasting other writers when he wrote:

As a Red for fourteen years and a redder Red after nearly four years of armying I suggest that 'Tory M.P. Gets the Verdict' was written by A. Debunker and not by A.B. Bunker.

Did 'Tory M.P. Gets the Verdict' because 'A Liberal Hit Out'? It seems to me that 'Libertas' wrote deliberately to disrupt the voters and let the Tories in.

Who is this 'Libertas', so liberal with his mis-statements, per-versions of facts and false assertions and so unliberal with having his name printed? Not a bit like the chap who says 'I am A. B. Bunker. Vote Tory'.

'Libertas' likens the trade unions to Big Business vested interests known as the Tory Party. He does not want to see the differences between the capitalists bent on amassing personal wealth and trade unions fighting for the workers' right to social security.

When peace comes, not a returned soldier will be employed unless the capitalists make a profit out of him; neither will he be employed if the capitalists make a bigger profit by not

Bhan cartoon from *Seac*.

"Are you sure the spoon's clean?"

employing the soldier and instead invest their money abroad exploiting cheap foreign and colonial labour.

After the last war Jarrow was murdered, the Clyde and Lancashire devastated because British capitalists found they made more profit by building their ships in Danzig and manufacturing their cotton in India.

After this war our tears, toil and sweat won't stop this exploitation, but socialism will.

Private Geldberg had high hopes, and except for a worried section of officers, 'red' was not a rude word at the time.

An officer cadet wrote to *Battle Dress* in 1940:

Battle Dress No. 1 was a great disappointment for a great many eager readers. A superior 'school mag' has resulted. The fourth form playing at newspaper reporters made its bow and kudos has been confined to two men – the editor and the most popular man in the O C T U.

Another writer to *Battle Dress* had a good deal to say about poetry. Though much of what he said was pompous and dogmatic, nevertheless some of the comments of this would-be officer who signed his letter 'Civil Servant' are worth noting:

I feel there was some good prose about the last war, which gave one an idea of the altered values of a soldier's life, when the quality and temperature of one's soup can become more important for a moment than the death of his friends. But the poetry was lousy, because poets kept harking back to the piping

56

The Eighth Army's *Crusader*, 1942.

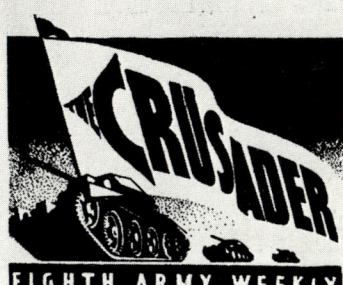

THE CRUSADER
EIGHTH ARMY WEEKLY

Issued to the Fighting Forces in the desert

No. 21 Vol. 2   September 21, 1942

Review for the Blue

RUSSIA

Bloodiest battle of war — the battle for Stalingrad still rages. West of city Nazis drove wedge in Russian defences, but efforts to widen this were defeated by persistent counter attacks. "Fight to last street, last house, last man," was appeal in Red Army paper, "Red Star." "Stalingrad is theatre of infernal battles never before experienced in history," said Berlin radio. Meanwhile battle grows in intensity without decision.

Biggest blow to Red Army on other fronts was fall of Novorossisk, Black Sea port. Conitnuing advance Nazis tried to cross Terak river, but were hurled back. Berlin claimed Germans were outnumbered in drive to oil of Grozni.

ENGLAND

Calling for further credit of £100,000,000 Chancellor Sir Kingsley Wood told House war had cost ten times that sum to date. He appealed for less personal expenditure and more saving not to jeopardise country's strong financial position.

MADAGASCAR

Allied forces in Madagascar went into action again because of Jap air activity over island and fear that submarines might menace our shipping in Mozambique channel. Under General Sir William Platt they quickly seized key points on west coast.

PACIFIC

After heavy fighting Aussie troops fell back to positions 44 miles from Port Moresby. Sydney newspaper says Japs are masters of jungle craft. They stay among trees and avoid all paths. Aussies have only sounds among trees as targets. Things comparatively quiet off Solomons this week. American dive and torpedo bombers claimed hits on Jap battleship and cruiser.

CHINA

Chinese claim successes in Nanachang where their Army is fighting in streets. At Kwangtung they pushed Japs back to where they were before May offensive. Japs stubborn resistence at Kinhwa neutralises for moment Chinese occupation of "bomb Tokyo" airfields of Chushsien and Lishui, which are too close to Chekiang capital to be used as bases.

SEA BORNE FORCE IN RAID ON TOBRUK

While Allied bombers carried out one of the largest scale night raids of the war on Tobruk on the night of September 13, sea-borne troops effected a landing at the port.

Damage was done to shipping, shipping facilities, stores and storehouses.

Our forces landed in face of strong opposition and inflicted casualties on the enemy before withdrawing. The withdrawal was not effected without losses, which in view of the strength of the defences, were to be expected.

Another light naval force successfully bombarded enemy lines of communication in the El Daba area. This force returned to harbour without loss or damage.

Land Operations

Land operations, up to the time "Crusader" went to press were confined to enemy artillery exchanges, particularly in the southern sector, where enemy positions and vehicle concentrations were shelled.

Heavy attacks on shipping and port installations at Benghazi, aerodromes at Sidi Heneish, and selected objects at Tobruk were carried out by heavy, medium and light bombers, causing explosions and fires.

Air activity over the battle area has been on a reduced scale.

The Army Commander surveys battle area from tank.
Photo W.P. Martin

Newcastle Honours Desert V.C.

The King has approved the award of the Victoria Cross to three members of the Middle East Forces for outstanding gallantry and devotion to duty. Two of the awards are posthumous.

The names of the new V.C's, an Englishman, an Australian and a South African are :

Private Adam Herbert Wakenshaw, Durham Light Infantry (posthumous).

Private Arthur Gurney, A.I.F. (posthumous).

Sgt. Quintin George Murray, U.D.F.

Newcastle is proud of Pte. Wakenshaw. Townspeople have already raised three hundred pounds to educate Tommy, aged seven, and Lilian, aged three, his orphaned kiddies.

Contact

VOL. 2, NO. 72   12 APRIL 1945.

Bell of St Paul's will ring V-E day out to the world

ONE of the biggest roles in smashing the German armies on the East bank of the Rhine and making possible the huge sweep into Western Germany has been played by the tactical air forces. Attack planes like this Typhoon, with bomb, cannon and rocket tore to shreds the German armoured concentrations and softened the opposition to a point where the land armies could rush irresistibly through the enemy defences.

FOURTEEN bellringers of Saint Paul's Cathedral, several of them more than 60 years old, will announce western victory to the world within an hour of the official declaration. Their first peals on the twelve great bells will be the signal to bellringers in churches all over Britain and indeed throughout the Empire to tell the people of the end of the European war.

The day on which the announcement is made and the next day will be public holidays in Britain. If the news comes early enough, there will be a thanksgiving service in St Paul's at noon: if it comes later, in the evening. There will be a great thanksgiving on the Sunday after the V-E Day.

The Home Office hope that by August the whole of Britain will be "lit up" in its full peacetime brilliance, says the Evening Standard. Except for Greater London and some areas on the East Coast, still subject to outside chances of raids from piloted aircraft, the whole country theoretically could now go on to full lighting. Practically there are difficulties. Local authorities are finding both men and materials for the switchover scarce. Because of this some authorities have decided to skip the intermediate stage of "moonlighting" and are going ahead with preparations for full lighting.

The Home Office consider and local authorities agree that there

IMPATIENT

WOKING, SURREY.—A crowded troop train south Coastward bound, stopped here recently. On one of the carriages was chalked up "To Berlin".

After some delay one impatient soldier stuck his head out of the window pointed to the chalk mark and yelled to the porter, "Hi cock, tell the engine driver to get blinking move on, will you, or we'll be late for the ruddy party."

would be a moral effect in the whole country switching over to full lighting on the same night. For this purpose a date will probably be fixed late in August. Towns and villages throughout Britain, many of them bombdamaged, are preparing to celebrate the big night with lights, dancing, and thanksgiving services.

ENSA AND THE STARS

Formby replies to Dean

THE recent statements by E.N.S.A. Director Basil Dean are commented on by George Formby and George Wood in a joint letter to "The Times". Referring to the criticism that the stars were only prepared to work in comfortable base areas, the letter says, "The fact is, of course, we have to go where ENSA sends us."

General Leese made it possible for Formby to go to Burma and Air Marshal Joubert arranged for Wood to go there, the letter says, adding "It is nonsense to suggest that they would pander to the artists by making it possible for them to have a special aircraft unless they saw good reasons for giving the actors such valuable transport."

"To say that the stars expected that the order of battle should be changed to suit their convenience is childish. We certainly have not suggested that our services were not wanted because we could not be accepted in the front line at a particular time."

"We did suggest that our services were wanted in forward areas and ENSA seemingly did not realise this."

80 P.C. PROXIES HOME FOR 1ST BY-ELECTION

Two thousand men and women in the Forces overseas have sent home proxies entitling their wives and parents to cast votes for them in the by-election at Motherwell, Lanarkshire, today. This is eighty per cent of the Service voters eligible.

The candidates are Alexander Anderson (Labour), and Dr. Robert McIntyre (Nationalist). The by-election is caused by the death of James Walker (Labour).

"NO AVOIDABLE DELAYS" IN RELEASE—BEVIN

FAR EAST MEN'S RIGHTS WILL BE SAFEGUARDED

"WHILE there must be no weakening until the war is finally cleared up in the Far East, all serving over there may be sure that their rights will be safeguarded. We have endeavoured to be fair to everybody and we are more than ever determined that Class 'B' releases will be strictly limited," said Ernest Bevin, Labour Minister at a Press conference announcing the issue of the Government handbook "Release and Resettlement" to every man and woman in the forces.

Twenty-five tons of the booklets are already on their way as a first consignment to the most distant theatres. More are following daily by sea, land and air. Deliveries of the booklets will begin in the Far East. An advance foretaste of the booklet is provided by the publication, in "Contact's" last, current, and next issues, of extracts from the handbook cabled out by the War Office.

"Once the Cease Fire takes place in Europe there will be a standstill period," Bevin told reporters. "Troops cannot be rushed out immediately after. The Service departments themselves will announce what groups will be released and discipline and order must be maintained if the scheme is to work properly.

"No exaggerations, please" the Labour Minister urged the Press. "We want no upsets, in the interests of the men and women concerned. There will be no avoidable delays, I assure you."

Bevin hinted that the building trade, agriculture, hospital services and similar important callings will be first out under Class "B", but emphasised releases would be very limited.

"Our main duty is to keep Class A as high as we can," he declared.

"The business broke down last time because people came out of their turn. This caused jealousy trouble and disaster among the soldiers and we are determined to prevent it this time.

"Large numbers of specialists must be kept in to fight the Japanese war, but men and women will be kept in against their will only in cases of absolute military necessity. The Services are co-operating whole-heartedly because, like me, they don't want discontented men. I do not fear any difficulties."

PAY BONUSES ARE CUT IN 'PEACE' FACTORIES

THE announcement that 19 Government-owned factories are to be allocated to civilian production heralds the beginning of the switch from war to peace production—and from war to peace wages, writes the "Daily Mail".

Most of the workers who go to these factories will be exchanging high wages for security.

Basic rates of pay for engineers and electrical workers, who will form the bulk of the workers, will remain the same. Increases of about 25 per cent in basic rates, negotiated by the Amalgamated Engineering Union and the Electrical Trades Union during the war, were permanent increases.

But the union members who go to the peace factories will sacrifice war bonuses, overtime, and special rates for Saturday afternoon and Sunday work.

Some of the personnel released from the munitions factories to go back to their old jobs in textiles in Yorkshire have reacted to this change by "moving-on" to other war factories, where they can continue to earn the high war-time wages.

Japanese Campaign pay for I.A.

JAPANESE campaign pay has now been authorized for all personnel of the Indian Army of the rank of Captain and below who are serving in Burma and eastwards, says a Press note.

This special pay will be given retrospectively with effect from November 1, 1944.

The change will mean an additional Rs. 69 a month for both British and Indian officers of or below the rank of Captain.

In the case of British other ranks the rates will be: 2s a day for warrant officers Class 1, 1s 9d a day for staff sergeants and 1s 6d a day for sergeants.

The above personnel serving in India or Ceylon will not receive Japanese Campaign Pay under the new scheme, but British officers of the Indian Army serving in India or Ceylon and drawing Indian Army allowance at rates lower than Japanese Campaign Pay will receive a compensatory allowance to make up the difference. Similar allowances will be granted to British other ranks of the India Unattached List.

Analogous concessions will be granted to corresponding ranks of the RIN, RIAF and RAF serving with the RIAF.

Yank Columnist praises the "Patient, Tough Tommy"

A tribute to the British soldier was paid today by Hanson W. Baldwin, columnist of the "New York Times". He devoted the whole of a thousand-word column to the British Tommy whom he described as a "patient, indomitable, tough little man".

"Until the crossing of the Rhine by the Twenty-first Army Group, troops of the United Kingdom who have fought this war from Burma to Germany have not recently been in Western front headlines," said Baldwin.

"But the Tommy has been fighting all the same. Many have been in uniform more than five and a half years. They have seen an end to their long trial by endurance."

Baldwin said the British infantryman is "less ebullient but perhaps more patient than the American." "The Tommy, gallant and enduring, already has hung his washing on the Siegfried Line" Baldwin concluded. "And now, deep in the Reich, he is still playing his full part in the final chapter of the war against Germany."

GIVE FORCES HOUSING PRIORITY, URGES TOWN PLANNING EXPERT

THE suggestion for a scheme for the allocation of houses to give ex-Servicemen an advantage is contained in a letter to the "Evening News" from John G. Martin, Secretary of the National Housing and Town Planning Council.

"Some local authorities have already announced that in the allocation of the municipal dwellings claims of members and ex-members of the Forces will be especially considered and the greatest priority given to those who have had long service or who have been discharged on account of wounds or other disabilities," he says.

"Unfortunately other authorities have adopted rules whereby all applicants (including ex-Servicemen) for their houses must have previously resided and or have been employed in the area concerned.

"Obviously such rules do not permit of much elasticity in a discharged man's choice of employment. Would it not be possible for the Prime Minister and the Ministry of Health to urge all local authorities to draw suitable schemes for the allocation of houses—possibly on the 'points' system which has worked so well in other spheres—whereby ex-Servicemen could be granted some advantage over other applicants?

Contact, April 1945, published in India and Ceylon.

times of peace, and thinking that larks were singing in England, instead of listening to the new songs round them. In the same way, English poets refused for a hundred years to recognise the industrial revolution and the modern city as the subjects of poetry. Eliot was the first to look *at* it instead of away from it. Who is to be the Eliot of modern war? Who is going to write about the new sights, sounds and smells the soldier knows, instead of going all bucolic about the Maginot Line? The only poetic remark I have heard about modern war was that of Mussolini's son who noticed that, if you dropped a bomb accurarately on a group of Abyssinians, 'They blossomed like a rose.' This is excellent. It shows an eye for a metaphor – which, as Aristotle said, is the poet's most important gift – and it is absolutely divorced from the attitude of the moralist, who thinks, attitudes

stifle some poetry, as you know, and the first poet who forgets that war is horrible and wicked will, I hope, be worth reading.

An unusual letter was one written to his mother by a German lance-corporal of 115 Panzer Grenadier Regiment, which formed part of the 15th Panzer Division in Rommel's unsuccessful offensive at El Alamein. The letter fell into the hands of *The Crusader*, which published it on 5 October 1942 under the caption, 'Wasser Bitte':

Many thanks for the packet of lemonade powder which you sent me. Unfortunately there was no water available to put it into, so I have had to eat it dry. It did relieve my thirst a bit, all the same. This lack of water is a frightful misery for us [*ein furchtbares Elend*]. I am glad to get a mouthful of rusty slush from the radiator of a derelict lorry. Our only hope of relief is to get to Alexandria; but unfortunately Tommy is putting up a very stiff resistance.

Letters to *Ceylon Review*, usually well written and informed, were often long and detailed and touched on all kinds of subjects: sponsored radio, the birth rate, and state control were some of the items dealt with. Coal gasification was the subject of one long letter which read in part:

. . . we of the working class read with satisfaction of the ultimate aim of the miners. Nationalisation of miners – that constitutes a step forward but plans, bold ones, laid down for the gasification of coal underground would transform that step forward into a leap to the benefit of all who work underground under the present terrible conditions.

Letters expressing petty jealousies and unit rivalries were plentiful, and writers often made much of their doubtful honours, such as who were really entitled to be called the 'bewhiskered veterans of Myitkyina', or which was the only regiment in the British army that

59

had been granted the privilege by special charter of marching backwards up the steps of St Paul's wearing deerstalkers at the alert and trousers at half mast. In 'Words for Weeds', the letter column in *Roundup*, Sgt. Chris Winkler stated:

> Dear *Roundup*. Every issue of the *Roundup* we read of some Engineering outfit being called 'bewhiskered veterans of Myitkyina'. Now don't think we want to get all the credit, but have you ever made an attempt to find out who made the glider landing at Myitkyina, who built this field and who kept it open during Japs, mud and shellfire?
>
> We are the Airborne Engineers. We built the strip so that the bewhiskered Engineers you mention could land here about six months after we did.
>
> You have a roving reporter; let him rove up here and find out the score.

Many servicemen saw film shows at garrison cinemas through mobile film units, and at local cinemas if they were fortunate enough to be stationed near to town, and they continued to take a lively interest in them. H. D. Kewley, Royal Signals, Field Regt. R.A. S.E.A.C., had this to say about film remakes in a letter to *Contact* in April 1945:

> A few days ago I saw Frank Sinatra in *Step Lively* and although the acting and the cast were excellent, I was disappointed to discover that I had seen the same plot and story about six years ago called *Room Service*. Groucho Marx played the role now played by George Murphy, while Sinatra's role was filled by Frank Albertson. This is becoming a common practice to make films under false titles. *Free, Blonde and 21* was remade as *Ladies of Washington*. *Outward Bound* is now *Between Two Worlds*, and many more. I'm sure a reissue would be appreciated much more than a remake. For example it is rumoured that *Scarface* is to be remade with Alan Ladd. Now who can forget the acting of Paul Muni in the original? It was a masterpiece, as was George Raft's portrayal of the coin-flipping bodyguard. He was the only *Scarface*. As a reissue it would be accepted readily, but a remake could never be a real success. Same with *Little Caesar*, *The Informer*, *Stagecoach* and many more memorable films. A few reissues would not be out of place and I'm sure there are quite a few who will agree.

Servicemen's letters showed that they preferred films with girls and 'plenty of legs' to films about the war, and this provoked controversy at times. The following two letters, the first from a captain in a Mobile Kinema Section and the other from a driver in the R.A., show that they were not on the side of the 'leg men':

> Capt. P. G. Lacey (*Seac*, 9 May) bemoans the fact that his unit has seen only two films in three months, *The Way Ahead* and *San*

POWER.

Demetrio, London. He says these films are civilian morale boosters, and not the type of film that goes down well in forward areas.

I think all of us take a suspicious view of semi-propaganda films, but *The Way Ahead* is a film of real entertainment value without the glamorous heroics, devoid of any reality, that some film companies put on the market. The same applies to *San Demetrio*.

Our mobile cinema section has shown the following leg and dance shows in the last few months: *Pin-up Girl*, *Girls He Left Behind*, *Melody Inn*, *Hit Parade of 1943*, *Sensations of 1945* and *Follow the Boys*. And of course, we have catered for those with, shall we say, a little more highbrow taste by *Song of Russia*, which has some lovely symphony works, *Fanny by Gaslight*, etc.

It is not possible at the present time for everyone to see all of these films owing to the fluid tactical situation and the rapid mobility of this campaign. Our Indian brothers-in-arms also deserve their fair share of films, which we are showing them.

My unit has just seen *Sensations of 1945*, an American extravaganza of music, gals, legs and sensation after sensation. I enjoyed pieces of it, but I found myself bewildered by jitter-bugging antics, dazed by rhythmic discord, and not particularly thrilled by lanes of lovely legs. This seemed to be a general reaction.

61

Next evening we saw *The Way Ahead*, a well-acted British film depicting the life (and what a life) of some British Tommies from 'Calling Up' to 'Mopping Up'. It was so realistic that we felt ourselves to be there on the screen.

Capt. Lacey would lead us to believe that girls, gags, and legs are wanted by troops fighting in Burma. For myself, I like first-rate British and American dramas – a mixed bag for mixed audiences.

Some writers took their films very seriously indeed. N. A. Forde wrote thus to *Ceylon Review*:

May I congratulate your correspondent George Walters on the evident catholicity of taste exemplified by his recent visits to the cinema, in which he appears to have covered virtually the entire range of culture, from what he considers the sublime to the similarly qualified ridiculous. Perhaps Mr Walters doesn't realise that the sublime and the ridiculous are relative values, however, and so I hesitantly suggest that he try to read Nietzsche on the subject.

I heard the barracking of Berlioz' 'Carnival Romaine' to which Mr Walters refers; a normally tolerant person might have been willing to charge it off to the Christmas festive season, and let it go at that. But as Mr Walters is obviously not normally tolerant,

I'd like to point out that the telephoto shots of the symphony orchestra exhibited the instrumentalists in a perspective which apotheosised the ridiculous far more than Mr Walters' quartet of crooners . . . with cretinous grins – who were at least not trying to be serious.

Mr Walters merits further congratulation on his adept use of the English language in his acidulous condemnation of the popular film. Mr Walters appeared quite inebriated with the exuberance of his own verbosity, to quote Disraeli; but in reality Mr Walters merely quoted a few of the bigoted clichés often used by the pseudo-intelligentsia who, having through their intellectual snobbery long lost the common touch, desperately endeavour to prove their own mental superiority by fatuous, jejune criticism of popular tastes.

Probably Mr Walters doesn't realise that by his synthetic outburst against popular appreciation of popular films, he inevitably classes himself with that vulgar, low-brow audience which gave Berlioz the bird, as well as with those elegant Parisians who booed Wagner's *Tannhauser*, and the critics who called Beethoven barbarous. Intolerance is never a virtue, not even in such an oracle as Mr Walters would be.

One also wonders why Mr Walters ever went to see the film which he deprecates with such pontifical fervour in Scene 1 of his letter. I can think of four possible reasons: 1, He is a manic depressive and must be amused no matter what it does to his intellect and emotions.

2, He can't read the advertisements and didn't know what he was in for – surely not true of a man of Mr Walters' evident erudition!

3, Someone gave him a free ticket.

4, No one ever told him.

Again, in the last para of his letter, Mr Walters refers to 'the mental attitudes of an 18-year old', later generously reducing that figure to 10 or 12. Yet Mozart and Menuhin had pretty fair attitudes at those ages – and if Mr Walters thinks that is begging the question, let me ask him by what system he measures mental attitudes (by which I presume he means Intelligence Quotients). I.Q.s must be measured by some system: and if Mr Walters doesn't know that, or can't be bothered, then obviously he doesn't know what he is talking about – Q.E.D.

The reply from R. James was short and not so sweet:

I am amused by the verbosity of the film critics who have been writing to your journal, particularly the effort of N. A. Forde who tears George Walters to pieces with gusto. According to Mr Forde, our good friend Walters, by giving the raspberry to crooners with cretinous grins, classes himself with the vulgar low-brow audiences who booed Wagner, Berlioz and Beethoven.

I have listened to many men talk in praise of crooners, jazz,

SEAC

THE SERVICES NEWSPAPER OF SOUTH EAST ASIA COMMAND

No 291 One Anna
THURSDAY, 26 OCTOBER, 1944.

Printed by Courtesy of THE STATESMAN in Calcutta.

Good Morning . . .

Strange and stimulating news item from SHAEF HQ in Paris—not this time news of war but may be a portent for the peace-makers.

The first German "democracy"—the quotation marks, very properly, are Reuter's—since Hitler came into power, is now said to be functioning within a few miles of Aachen. Its inhabitants are some 6,000 civilians removed behind the American lines after the town's surrender.

An official eye is naturally kept on this political experiment by Allied Military Government Control, but the machinery of self-government is solely German. At its head is the former Vice-Burgomaster of Aachen, helped by a representative body of citizens.

And there aren't any Nazis not anywhere there—in so far at least as a quick check-up has discovered. Not any of the more rabid variety, certainly.

*

But according to the report, there *are* some Jews. They are being well-treated by the others "with whom they appear to get along well." Our quotation marks this time.

It occurs to this writer that if he were one of the 6,000 citizens of Aachen living under the eye of an invader, one of whose cardinal purposes was to secure freedom for the oppressed—Jew and non-Jew alike—he too would "appear to get along well" with Jews.

There is a saying to the effect that when the Devil was sick, the Devil a monk would be.

However maybe that is the way it goes in the new democratic state that was Aachen. Maybe we have the virgin material here to prove that there are two kinds of Germans, "good" Germans and Nazis. And maybe, again, we haven't.

*

Let us give a little thought to the background of this strange grasping, non-co-operative people. Let us discard, however, regretfully the amiable theory that they are all direct descendants of Attila, the Hun. Even if Attila had owned a bicycle, his blood strain must have worn thin by now.

Perhaps we can more properly give blame to Frederick the Great and his Prussians. In common English usage if we wish to describe a greater degree of barbarism we term it 'Prussian' barbarism. There's much in a name.

Nearer to our times come Bismarck, ruthless Empire builder, and the wood-chopper of Doorn, as fanatical to destroy it. For 50 years before World War I, Blood and Iron dominated Germany and the German people.

For five years before World War II "Guns Before Butter" ruled their children.

*

In this almost unbroken century of militarism and aggression we look hard for any seed of democracy. The end of World War I thought that it had found one with the overthrow of the Hohenzollerns and the establishment of a Socialist republic.

Short-lived, ill-fated, trusted by no one and trusting none, the republic fell an easy prey first to the Army then to National-Socialism and Hitler. It was doomed to fail because the German people were not educated for democracy, and because their leaders were, for the most part, like blindfold children groping in a darkened room.

Maybe from the small beginning of 6,000 citizens of Aachen we can change all this. But the training will be a long one and the new lessons slowly learned.

Dr. Goebbels invented a dreadful verb—to Coventrate. After we have dealt with the Doctor and his filthy crew, perhaps we can turn the tables and Aachenize.

NEW MOVE IN ROCKE CASE

LONDON, Wed.—In the House of Commons yesterday the War Minister was asked if the text of broadcasts delivered by Lt.-Col. C. Rocke on behalf of the Italian Fascist Government were included in the information in this case submitted to the Director of Public Prosecutions.

Sir James Grigg replied "The text of one broadcast delivered by Col. Rocke on 15 July 1940 was included in information submitted to the Director of Public Prosecutions."

There was a broadcast in 1943 of which the Director of Public Prosecutions knew but had not the text condemning the attitude of Britain over sanctions.

Col. Rocke, a British officer living in Rome in retirement, was reported early in July to be held by Allied authorities pending investigation of his part in the Fascist broadcasting organisation in the early stages of Britain's war with Italy.—Reuter.

ITALY GAINS IN TOUGH FIGHTING

ROME, Wed.—The Fifth Army has maintained progress despite most determined resistance. American troops have taken Monte Belmonte.

British troops of the Fifth Army have captured the important height of Monte Spaduro.

Eighth Army infantry, supported by tanks, are advancing astride the main Bologna-Rimini road towards the Bevano.

JAPS SNIPE AND SHELL 5 DIV.

KANDY, Wed.—Today's SE Asia Command communiqué reports no major change from any sector of the Chin Hills or Arakan fronts.

On the Tiddim-Fort White road the Fifth Indian Division remains in contact with the enemy near Kennedy Peak. Japanese snipers are active, and there was some shelling. Our own guns have harassed enemy troop movement on the road.

In Northern Burma there was heavy patrol action by British troops in the railroad corridor south of Mohnyin. Chinese troops continued patrolling south of Kazu.

Aircraft of Eastern Air Command yesterday attacked targets on the Chindwin front, bombing positions in Kalemyo and Pinlebu areas, rivercraft on the Chindwin, and objectives in the Myittha Valley.

Heavy bombers caused large fires during a night attack on dumps at Taungup.

Burma Air Step-up: Back Page.

THEY COVER THE BATTLEFRONTS

LONDON, Wed.—The War Secretary in the Commons today gave figures of Allied war correspondents covering the various battlefronts.

On the western front, he said, the Empire had 124 correspondents and the US 177; in the Mediterranean there were 47 Empire and 63 US correspondents and in South East Asia 32 from the Empire and 10 from the US.

AIR DELEGATION

WASHINGTON, Wed.—A Philippines delegation will attend the International Civil Aviation Conference in Chicago.—Reuter.

JAPS CUT NEWS

LONDON, Wed.—The Japanese News Agency reported today that Japanese newspapers will be limited to two pages daily after 1 November.—Reuter.

HANOVER BOMBED

LONDON, Wed.—Last night the RAF attacked Hanover and Western Germany.

Jap Carrier Sunk, 2 Others Hit

BIGGEST NAVAL BATTLE OF WAR RAGING

PEARL HARBOUR, Wed.—In the biggest naval battle of the war, a large Jap aircraft carrier has been sunk, and damage caused to two other big carriers, five or six battleships, a cruiser, and several unidentified warships in a three-pronged battle with the American Third Fleet near the Philippines.

This is announced in a communiqué today from Admiral Chester Nimitz, C-in-C of the Pacific. It says that the US light carrier Princeton was sunk by American ships after being badly crippled and her magazines had exploded. The captain and 1,360 officers and men were saved.

The action began on Monday afternoon (US time), extended throughout yesterday and, says the communiqué, general action is continuing.

Princeton was attacked by a large force of land-based Japanese planes. About 150 were shot down during the attack.

The American Fleet forced the Japanese Fleet to action and inflicted severe damage, says Reuter's special correspondent.

So far there have been three main actions. On Monday morning planes of the US Third Fleet patrolling west of the Central Philippines saw three or four battleships, 10 cruisers and 13 destroyers steaming from the west.

100 B-29's In Raid

They attacked at once near Mindoro Island. By yesterday all the Jap battleships had been damaged by bombs and a battleship and a cruiser were torpedoed from the air.

The second enemy force—two battleships, one cruiser and four destroyers—was sighted and attacked from the air 200 miles to the south and by yesterday each ship was damaged.

The third force, the only one with aircraft carriers, was sighted heading towards the Philippines from Japanese home waters. American carrier-based planes engaged it south-east of Formosa. One carrier was sunk and two others severely damaged.

Incomplete reports indicate more severe damage. The battle continues with the Americans determined to smash Japanese sea power now that they have been forced to an open fight.

While the battle was reported to be in progress, a strong force of China-based Super-fortress bombers attacked the island of Kyushu, southernmost island of Japan proper, the fourth raid on the island since 21 August.

Airfield Taken

Japanese Imperial HQ announced that the raid, which lasted an hour and a half, was made by about 100 aircraft.

The Japanese said Saishu island was also attacked.

San Pablo airfield, in the Philippines, is in Allied hands.

A field dispatch from Tacloban, capital of Leyte island, reported that American forces have crossed the narrow San Juanito strait and established a bridghead on Samar island.

The Japanese near Palo, on Leyte, are still resisting stubbornly, but their positions are being reduced.

In the last two days the Japanese have made desperate counter-attacks, but have been forced back with heavy losses.—Reuter.

35 MILES TO KOENIGSBERG

LONDON, Wed.—Red Army columns, by-passing German infantry and armoured groups, have broken through the second East Prussian defence line, according to Moscow Radio's correspondent in East Prussia.

In a major engagement, more than 120 self-propelled guns and tanks were destroyed and 3,000 Germans killed.

The Germans have sent four tank divisions to try to stem the attack. They include a "Greater Germany" SS division and fresh infantry and special units, with the order "throw every Russian off German soil or die where you stand."

The Soviet invasion armies are now only 35 miles from Koenigsberg, East Prussian capital, says Reuter, and General Cherniakhovsky, Russian Commander, is packing more and more troops into the 90-mile Insterburg gap in the German lines.

Troops Storm Gap

The hard crust of German border fortifications, with three-storey Maginot type forts has been decisively broken and the Red Army is driving to reach Koenigsberg before the Germans have time to regroup and move up fresh reinforcements.

The main body of the invasion armies, led by 60 generals, is already over river Raminte below Gumbinen.

As the Russians advance into East Prussia they enter an eerie, deserted land, with cottage doors swinging in the wind to reveal tables set for abandoned meals, clocks still ticking in houses from which the occupants had fled only a few hours before.

TANKS CLOSE IN ON LOST LEGION

LONDON, Wed.—Russian tank spearheads are closing in on Kirkenes in Northern Norway, the main supply base of the lost Austrian Alpine Legion which retreated from Finland.

Kirkenes is also the main base of the Luftwaffe's Fifth Air Fleet.—Globe.

BRIDGE-BUSTING

USAAF Mitchells of Eastern Air Command have knocked out the railway bridge at Hsipaw, 100 miles north-east of Mandalay, on the main line to Lashio, and damaged another bridge, farther west.

Mitchells destroyed a bridge between Mandalay and Yeu.

HUNTING THE JAP DOWN ARAKAN WAY :—Indian troops of 26 Div searching a village for Jap stragglers after defeating the enemy attack on Goppe Bazaar.

FIGHTING BY SEARCHLIGHT

SHAEF, Wed.—Searchlights are being used to provide artificial "moonlight" during street fighting in Hertogenbosch, the communications centre between Nijmegen and Utrecht which is now largely in Allied hands.

One of Gen Dempsey's columns is racing north-west from Eisch to cut the main Hertogenbosch-Tilburg road now less than 2,000 yards away.

All the northern part of Hertogenbosch has been cleared and many Allied patrols are across the Zuid Willems Canal in the southern part of the town.

Line Caving In

Breskens is still in British hands. A report that we had withdrawn is officially said to be inaccurate.

British Second Army troops are reported to be smashing the defences on a 12-mile front in Holland.

A new blow brought about the swift capture of the German stronghold of Best, south-east of Hertogenbosch and a number of other places. There are indications that the Germans are pulling back all along the line, which has "begun to cave in."

Gen Dempsey's new attack moved so fast that two bridges over the River Maler were captured intact and British troops are reported to be less than 10 miles from Tilburg.

Escape Cut Off

Away on the west, Canadian troops, after days of bitter fighting, cut the Germans' narrow escape route and isolated troops on Walcheren Island.

Gen Eisenhower's communiqué today states that south of Breskens the area from Schoondijke to Oostburg is in our hands and Allied troops are on the edge of Oostburg.

In the area north of Aachen and Luneville there were no substantial changes.—Reuter.

NO BARGAINING WITH THE AXIS

LONDON, Wed.—Mr Churchill told the Commons today that unconditional surrender in the sense of no bargaining with the enemy was still the policy of the British Government. The three-Power declaration of 12 May to the Axis satellites should also be borne in mind, he said.

Churchill was answering a question by Sir Thomas Moore (Cons, Ayr Burghs) who asked how the policy of unconditional surrender was reconciled with the system by which former enemies had under military pressure changed sides and were now apparently Allies.—Reuter.

FRANCE OUT OF SECURITY TALKS

WASHINGTON, Wed.—President Roosevelt said yesterday that France would not be included immediately in the post-war security talks.

A message from London says China, Colombia, Peru and the Republic of Haiti have recognised the French Provisional Government.—Reuter.

TITO TAKES MAIN LINE TOWN

LONDON, Wed.—The Free Yugoslav Radio reports that Marshal Tito's forces have captured Novisad, a junction of the main line from Belgrade to Budapest.

The ancient port of Petrovaradin, on the southern bank of the Danube, has also been captured.—Reuter.

GREECE SPEED-UP

ROME, Wed.—British troops have advanced north of Dhomokos, already captured, and patrols are 40 miles south of Larissa, Central Greece's most important road and rail junction.

150 LOCOS SHOT UP

LONDON, Wed.—Four hundred Allied fighter planes shot up 150 locomotives and 400 cars between Hamburg and Kassel yesterday.—Reuter.

HELLCAT'S 31 TO 1

WASHINGTON, Wed.—The U.S. Navy is now using in the Pacific the new Hellcat which has a speed of over 400 miles an hour. The aircraft is bringing down Jap aircraft at a ratio of 31 to one.—Reuter.

How *Seac* looked in 1944.

The American General, SEAC: Lt. General Dan Sultan, Commander, Northern Area Combat Command. He led Chinese, Britons, Indians and Americans.

and modern rhythmic music – but I have not till now come across one who classes with the works of Wagner and Beethoven, the pot-boiling commercial dance tunes with which the average film is encumbered.

Does Mr Forde think that in a hundred years time the tunes of, say, Jerome Kern, will be regarded as the works of a genius? Really, Mr Forde, come off it.

A film that stirred up a hornets' nest was *Objective Burma*, starring Errol Flynn. Servicemen protested vehemently against the showing of the film, especially those in S.E.A.C. A letter to *Seac* from an American pilot said it all. The pilot was Lieut.-Col. William H. Taylor, Jr., of the U.S.A.F. One of the world's leading glider pilots, he was C.O. of the glider men under Cochran in the Wingate expedition and was later sent to England to brief the American and British glider crews for D-Day. For his work he received an immediate award of the D.S.O. His letter to *Seac* was published in full in May 1945:

I recently saw a fairly new Warner Brothers' film called *Objective Burma*. It was shown before an audience of A.A.F. and R.A.F. officers and men at an Eastern Air Command base and presumably will have a wide distribution in India, possibly even in Burma.

It is a disturbing thought that this meretricious hodgepodge, which implies that Burma was invaded and liberated by a force of American parachutists, American glider-borne troops, two Gurkha guides and a Chinese officer, will be seen by thousands of men of the Fourteenth Army, who know better.

The thought that it has already been seen by millions of American civilians, whose impression of the Burma campaign must consequently be irreparably and viciously garbled is enraging.

The thought that it may have been seen by the mothers, fathers, friends and relatives of the many Allied troops – British, Indian, West African and Burmese – who lost their lives in the slow, painful struggle to clear Burma of the Japanese invader is sickening.

If no references to actual figures and events had been incorporated in the picture, one could accept it merely as a rather unfortunate attempt to provide entertainment. But by incorporating a number of feet of combat film and making free use of names and photographs of several notable commanders in South East Asia, the men who concocted *Objective Burma* produced an effect of having told the story of an actual operation, and in this manner not only mislead every theater-goer who is unfamiliar with the recent campaign in Burma, but jeopardize the close and happy inter-Allied relationships which made its success possible.

To me, a former participant in the Wingate-Cochran operation,

'Actually, Joe, we should thank our lucky stars we ain't stagnating with some static unit in Delhi.' Frolik cartoon from *Seac*.

the names Mountbatten, Stilwell, Wingate and Cochran, as used in this film, represent more than the men who bear or bore them. I'm sure that many other veterans of the Wingate-Cochran show, as well as members of the public in general, will feel the same way.

Those names have a fuller meaning. Each represents the many good soldiers who fought under those various commands. Stilwell represents thousands of Allied soldiers – Chinese, British and American.

Wingate, used in this manner, is just another name for the Chindits, for Scots, English, Africans, Indians, Americans, Burmese.

66

Cochran, in this film, plays no role as an individual; the glimpse one has of him implies that the American troops one sees in the movie are members of his Air Commandos and that their activities reproduce historic Air Commando operations.

Having written letters of condolence to the families of boys who lost their lives while serving under my command in the operations presumably depicted in *Objective Burma*, I can imagine with sympathy their feelings if they had the misfortune to witness this travesty of the truth.

As one of the Americans (who, contrary to the film, were in the minority in these particular operations) privileged to fight alongside our Allies in Burma, I am embarrassed by the implications of this film and revolted by the use of names and figures to obtain a spurious air of authenticity for this piece of fiction – a pseudo authoriticity, of commercial advantage to the producers and authors, that was obtained at the expense of very real 'blood, sweat and tears'.

Sometimes someone completely out of touch with popular thinking, or a relic of bygone days, would write to the press and be blasted from all sides for his trouble. One such letter was published in *Seac* with the inevitable consequences. On 14 August 1945, *Seac* published the following statement:

No letter published in *Seac* has aroused so much feeling as that in last Wednesday's issue from Capt. E. L. James headed 'Salvo'. Up to last night we had received 140 replies from officers and men, many carrying the names of five to fifty signatories. Not one agreed with Capt. James.

Before going any further, let's get this straight. This is not a controversy of Officer v. O.R., Volunteer v. Conscript, or Regular v. Conscript. It is a case of an individual expressing his own opinion – an opinion which in these days is in an infinitesimal minority. After reading all the letters sent us, we would say it is almost a case of Capt. James v. The World.

In view of the interest aroused, we print at length a hard-hitting reply from Cpl. John Hollington, as well as a large number of extracts from other letters.

From Corporal John A. Hollington:

My first impression on reading Capt. James's 'Salvo' was that he had joined the select band of humorists who, through the medium of your pages, are helping to keep up the morale of the troops in South East Asia. On second thoughts it struck me that his tone was too offensive to be funny and too spiteful to be ignored.

In the days of peace I was a civilian and as such paid taxes in support of the military force of which Capt. James is a member.

67

Theoretically, the armed forces of a nation are maintained to defend that nation. But this doesn't work out in practice, and when war is declared millions of civilians like myself are 'dragged in' to do a job which should come much easier to men of Capt. James's calibre and experience. At the time of my own 'dragging in' I thought nothing of gratuities and at the present time even less of them.

Capt. James suggests that 75 per cent of the men who are now fighting for their King and Country are doing so under duress. This is a beautiful morsel for the propagandists of Germany and Japan to get their teeth into.

I agree with Capt. James that if a country is worth living in it is worth fighting for. But may I ask that gentleman if pre-war Jarrow was a place worth living in and fighting for? Were the derelict areas of South Wales and the slums of East London worth fighting for? Are poverty and hunger worth fighting for?

Capt. James, running true to form, discovers that same old maggot in the military apple. It is lack of discipline, both mental and physical, which causes 'Jack' to imagine he is as good as his 'Master' and which leads him to expect equal treatment in the postwar England when he has once more made it safe for democracy.

This lack of discipline causes people like myself to have odd illusions and to imagine that, at times, Jack can be better than his master. In this matter we must not be tempted to use your correspondent as a standard by which to measure Jack's ability, for this gentleman, having reached his captaincy after only 20 years in the army, is an exception.

Capt. James is shocked by the bad turn-out and deportment of the 'specimens' who parade Calcutta's popular main thoroughfare. These officers and men who look like tramps are mainly from the forward areas and have not had time to smarten up their Burma hats or remove the anti-typhus stains from their well-worn patched battledress before availing themselves of leave, that 'amenity without which they seem incapable of doing their duty'. Such an appearance may be good enough when they burst, bloody and dusty, into Mandalay but it is not quite the thing for Chowringhee where it is likely to shock Capt. James.

A long way east of Chowringhee I once saw some of these 'specimens' who are the cause of the war dragging on to its sixth year. Some of them might have saluted if they had had a right arm, and I have no doubt their deportment would have been excellent could they have raised their broken bodies from the stretchers. I am sure their eyes would have lit up with holy joy if some kind person had told them that a grateful country was giving them £30-odd when it was all over. But some had no eyes.

Do not print this letter if you believe there is no decency

'Now the Missus 'ere is the Jap, see . . .' *Seac*.

left in the heart of the fighting man. Do not print it if you think there are no men left who are able to place ideals above a few pounds from a grateful country. Print it if you believe there are still officers who respect and are respected by the men who fight under them in those places a long long way from Chowringhee.

And for those who don't come back, write an epitaph, 'They died fighting against the worst evil that ever threatened mankind' – and leave it to Capt. James to chalk underneath 'but their saluting was atrocious'.

From nine R.A.F. men:

The Regular Army, the Territorial Army and Captain James's army, are no more. We are all in this struggle, professional soldiers, volunteers and conscripts alike.

The peacetime soldier has seen many changes – air liaison, mechanisation, enhanced prospects of promotion, and a flood of amateur soldiers who have no interest in soldiering as a career but only a desire to help win the war as quickly as possible.

Few of us have had much opportunity of studying the military aspect of Chowringhee – we have been otherwise engaged.

From Cpl. N. Pollard:

Capt. James appears to think of the B.O.R. as unintelligent, lacking initiative and possessing no capabilities. Has it not occurred to him that in civilian life the O.R. is, in many cases, the 'master' and the officer the 'Jack', to quote his own expression?

Whether officer or O.R., time spent in the Service is a 'cut'

69

'Okay, Sarge. Pin's out, lever's up, now what?' *Seac.*

from normal life, and gratuities should be paid on an equal basis.

From Sgt. H. Gonsalves:

Many 'conscripts' were engaged on work which the Government in its wisdom deemed to be of national importance for a period prior to their call-up. Does the Capt. not know that the authorities at home definitely discouraged volunteering at the beginning of the war, since they had already worked out a comprehensive plan to utilise Britain's manpower to the most effective advantage?

The conscript may have a certain contempt for the 'Balaclava' mentality of the Captain, but few of us would deny the great work put in by our small but efficient Regular Army in '39–40.

With regard to those 'specimens' regarded as tramps – it is to be

70

hoped that the Captain is aware that the great majority of these men have been fighting in the jungles of Burma for several years, where saluting and polished brasses have little effect on our fanatical enemy. Their appearance in Chowringhee is generally limited to fourteen days – which must be of some consolation to our diehard Captain.

The gunner who wrote the following did not earn himself many friends, nor did he influence many people. His letter was headed 'Gentleman Mosley'.

I am very pleased the rabble has ceased its cry regarding Sir Oswald Mosley. The scenes in London as published in the Press seemed reminiscent of the French Revolution when the blood-thirsty cry of the scum was '*à la guillotine*'. Mosley was released not only because his health suffered, but because he was not proven guilty of any crime against his country's war effort.

When we lived in the days of free speech his beliefs were at least sincere and he felt that the initiative of the British was on the wane. He wanted to create a Britain free of certain social evils, and to reincarnate the Drakes and other pioneers of our Empire.

England is great today because of the outspoken pioneers of yesterday, and so it is I remember Mosley – not as an anarchist but an idealist, a gentleman of courage, a great orator and patriot.

Sgt. M. Davies and Cpl. S. Priestley were not so enamoured of Fascists. They wrote a joint letter:

We read with disgust the report in *Seac* (8 July) quoting a *Daily Mirror* reporter – 'U.K. Fascists Come Back'. Arthur Winn, a former member of the British Union of Fascists, admits quite calmly that they have had an organisation all through the war, but kept underground. Now they are awaiting orders from their 'leader'. He also admits that their organisation has made full preparations to hold meetings and to carry on just as they did before the war.

As Servicemen now serving in Burma, we feel we must voice a loud protest that a Fascist Party is allowed to exist in Britain.

The captain who wrote the next letter was naive, optimistic, mealy-mouthed, or just plain obtuse:

Your correspondents appear to believe the British Union of Fascists should be stamped out, that their functions should be made illegal. I do not agree.

To suppress them by law would be to violate the rights of free speech and free congregation of the Briton. Rights I don't want to see meddled with in any way.

Apparently, the would-be suppressors don't have much faith in the British people. As if the B.U.F. could gain a hold and grow into a menace after six years of war against a Fascist enemy!

The type that wants to be a Blackshirt after this war won't be defeated by suppressive or restrictive measures, but by a really Better Britain.

Sergeant Murphy was naturally bewildered when the Italians changed sides after their defeat. He asked:

Can you tell me without disclosing any closely guarded military secrets just what is meant by a recent paragraph in the Press concerning 'due recognition to the Italian Patriot Army'? Who are these Italian patriots?

Not so very many months ago we were at war with Italy, going at them tooth and nail in the Western Desert and in Abyssinia. A lot of good lads from the old country have found desert graves from the bullet of an Italian rifle.

We shall soon have Free Italians, and Free Germans. We are certainly a big-hearted nation.

Cigarettes and tobacco were big concerns of the serviceman, and when it came to issues and brands of cigarettes for his welfare, there was a lot to be desired. He was usually most vociferous on that score, which will not surprise anybody who had to smoke V's or Lions, rotten at their best but by the time the soldier received them, damp and mildewy, well and truly past it. However, most soldiers considered they were better than no smokes at all, even though they complained bitterly. A warrant officer wrote:

The British Lion greets us with a Lion cigarette. Lions have strength – don't we know it!

They now have the audacity to issue even worse cigarettes than V's to fellows who are doing the scrapping, to fellows not within miles of a canteen who cannot even buy other cigarettes.

A man who is suffering the hardships and privations of the front line should be given the best his country can give.

We will not comment on the good fortune of some of our closest Allies in this theatre of war – good luck to them – but we are more than disgusted with the issue of these Lions. If we dared give these to Jap prisoners they would raise a cry against the brutal treatment of the British.

Maybe the British Museum would like a packet just as they wanted V's. They can have all our issues, administered to the British Public. I'm sure they would Salute the Soldier for attempting to smoke them.

PS: Got a fag, guv?

PPS: Flash! V's are still being issued to our forward troops. Proof can be given.

A lance-bombardier wrote:

Have just read in a *Seac* that some troops are complaining

'Sorry, sir, we've only
De Reszke!' Nicholson
cartoon from *Seac* reflecting
the scarcity of cigarettes.

about Lion cigarettes. Why? We lads up here at the front would
be pleased to see any sort of cigarette as we are *out*, *right out*,
so if you have any to spare, send the lot up here, and they will
be very welcome.

Failing this, how about setting the machinery to see that we get
as many cigarettes as we *need*. It's not a lot to ask, or is it?

Meanwhile a poor R.E. captain had his own troubles. Cigars were
his problem. His letter was a warning to all troops who smoked
Havanas:

A box of cigars marked 'Corona' was recently sent as a soldier's
gift to the United Kingdom. It was stopped by the Customs
authorities on the grounds that the title infringed the registered
mark in U.K. of 'La Corona', the product of the Havana Cigar
and Tobacco Factories Ltd. They made an exception on this
occasion provided that the offending marks i.e. 'Special Corona
de Luxe' and 'Churchill Corona de Luxe' were obliterated.

73

Would you please publish the information in order that everyone may be warned of this risk of confiscation. This would seem to apply also to other Indian products whose marks coincide with registered marks in U.K.

FASHION FRENZY
MODELLED BY Professor Phlitt (Burma's Beau Brummel)
1942 1944 1945

michael storm

The changing state of men's fashion: Michael Storm cartoon from *Seac*.

A cross section of the vast collection of letters written to service publications in World War II will best illustrate the diversity of subjects, military and otherwise, touched upon: the attitudes and thinking of regular soldiers and the vast army of civilian soldiers who bore the brunt of the war – officers and men who came from all walks of life to take up all sorts of unfamiliar martial tasks and found themselves posted all over the world to serve, wherever sent, in any designated capacity. For most it was the luck of the draw. Most made the best of it; most made virtues out of necessities; most did their allotted tasks well. But they wrote home about it – and they wrote to their papers, their own service papers.

From Gunner Thornton:

For Sgt. Buckland, Spr. Ganner and numerous others, Jazz is a language. Derived from the negro spirituals and blues it thrived in the gin mills and saloon bars of New Orleans and Chicago, expounded by virtuosos like 'Pine Top' Smith, and King Oliver. They played their music – from the urge in their soul.

Gradually jazz talent or some of it migrated to New York, here to be seized by certain gentry who foresaw its possibilities as a 'new' brand of music to be commercialised and scored for white tastes. Consequently Hail Swing with its synthetic blues and affected scores.

74

Call this brand of music, commercial swing, dance or anything – but not Jazz, the music of the Negro!

From L/Cpl. N. Ellis:

Regarding gratuities, why such a marked distinction between ranks? We have all come into the fray for the one job. Higher ranks are drawing big money, out of which they are able to save for their return to civilian life.

Help us to regain our feet when we leave the Army but give each, including women's services, an even break. A good many of the 'lower deck' held higher appointments and moved in higher circles before joining up – and will, no doubt, return to them.

From P. G. Rogers:

The Government's proposal to pay 'post-war tax-free gratuities' to members of the Services on a basis of *rank* and length of service is not compatible with the principles of democracy.

Would it not be a patriotic gesture on behalf of the Government if the scale of gratuities was revised to read:

75/- for each month of Service for O.R.s up to rank of Sgt.

50/- for each month of Service for Warrant Officers.

25/- for each month of Service for Officers up to rank of Major.

10/- for each month of Service for Lt/Col and above.

It would be by way of a little recompense to the average B.O.R. who has been receiving the 'knotty end of the stick' for the past five and a half years.

From L /Lt. F. W. McGeachy, Cameron Highlanders:

The attack on the bagpipes by your alleged Scottish correspondent cannot go unanswered. I do not believe that 'S.S.' is a Scot; if he is, he has probably never lived in Scotland. He is so woefully ignorant of the Scottish spirit.

He says the bagpipes are not truly the national instrument of Scotland because they are not Scottish in origin. What has the origin of the instrument got to do with it? Now, and for hundreds of years, the pipes are and have been the Scottish national instrument.

I wonder what instrument he thinks the truly national one – the saxophone?

I admit that the best setting for the pipes is not the drawing room, but to say that the pipes are imperfect in scale and harsh in tone is sheer nonsense. Played well, there is no more expressive instrument in existence.

What Scotsman has not thrilled to the inspiration of the march, the beauty of the pibroch, the laughter and joy of the jig, the sadness of the lament? There are pipe tunes to suit every mood.

75

Perhaps to the non-Scot the pipes sound a bit foreign, but I do object to a Scotsman running down an instrument steeped in Scottish tradition, its every note breathing all that is best in Scottish spirit and life and inciting the greatest happiness in the Scottish heart. Such conduct is heresy of the deepest dye.

"He's the whitest man I know!"

A Blimpish cartoon from *Jambo*.

From a corporal, S.E.A.A.F.:

In 'Good Morning' (*Seac*, 25 Aug) you state that the Japs have a racial superiority complex, that they treat all other people contemptuously and deceive themselves. Many B.O.R.s and British officers treat Indians in the same contemptuous manner, and equally deceive themselves. Ask an I.O.R. in any R.A.F. unit and you will get the answer.

We I.O.R.s are working with B.O.R.s, doing the same job and putting in the same amount of work. Yet what a difference in our pay and privileges.

We have no love for Jap Imperialism and arrogance. Neither have we any love for British Imperialism and arrogance.

From a L.A.C., S.E.A.A.F.:

I am an Indian airman serving in a forward area. Although I work and eat with British airmen, I do not enjoy the other facilities offered to them. I feel so awful at times, particularly in this place where civilisation seems like something left behind.

'Indian airmen can't do this, can't do that' seems to be the order of the century.

Recently the W.V.S. opened a canteen of sorts where one can get a drink and a few eats. Even this canteen is unapproachable to us.

76

'Destination secret – Eating irons will be handed in: chopsticks drawn in lieu.'
Seac.

There is no place where I can spend a couple of hours enjoying a drink. I did not expect this colour bar from W.V.S. organisers.

From Q.M.S. W. Whicker, R.E.:

Very frequently we men of the jungle open up our paper and are reminded of civilisation by a picture of some ravishing American actress or 'Pin-up' girl.

We all appreciate these tasty morsels so far from our reach, but why not let us see a little more of our own English beauties?

In Britain today, despite the fact that many are working in factories, the normal everyday girl still holds her own, even though strictly rationed on cosmetics. To prove this I am enclosing a photograph of a Taunton lassie who at the outbreak of war was 11 years old. Today she is 16, but oh boy; what an example of English beauty.

Up here she's an R.E. 'Pin-up' girl.

From Maj. R. H. Elliott and five other officers:

While it is appreciated that P.O.W.s have been through hell, have they gone through any greater hell than the average B.O.R.

77

AND NOW TO FINISH THE JAPS

Victory in Europe. To men fighting and working in Burma and India this great day represents the end of a monstrous tyranny and a mighty advance on the road to Victory in the East. Our war goes on—Japan must be beaten. Here, in V-Day messages, men who lead and direct the war in South East Asia outline the way of our future progress. "Next," says the Supreme Allied Commander, "it will be our turn for victory."

*

They're on the run

From Lord Louis Mountbatten, Supreme Allied Commander.

I HAVE today broadcast to those in the European theatre on behalf of the Allied forces in the South East Asia Command.

I have told them that I know I can speak for the men and women of every Service and of every Nation represented in this Command, when I express our gratitude to all those who, by their courage and devotion and sacrifices, contributed to making this great triumph possible; and that we out here feel the same pride today in their triumph as if it were our own.

I have told them that although we ourselves were busy taking on the Japanese, there was not a sailor, soldier or airman in South East Asia who did not follow every scrap of news about them and their battles that came to us by newspaper or by radio.

We were anxiously watching their progress in good times and bad; but we all had complete confidence in them and we knew it was only a matter of time before they would smash their way through to victory. I have told them that we thought about them a lot, and not only about those of them who were in the actual fighting areas.

We also thought of those who carried on in unsensational routine jobs, as Servicemen and women in stores and offices and workshops; and those who put in long, hard hours in factories, through the Blitz, V1 and V2, to keep the fighting troops supplied with the necessities of war; and those in the occupied countries, who resisted the invader at the risk of their lives.

I have reminded them that although Nazi Germany and Fascist Italy are now destroyed, the last enemy still remains.

We out here, who know we are fighting because there can be no lasting peace until the Axis is finally destroyed, have proved that we are superior in quality to the enemy. The Japanese are formidable fighters; yet in Burma this year we have outmanoeuvred and outfought them on their own chosen ground, where their propaganda had claimed they were invincible. And now they are on the run.

Next, it will be our turn for victory!

Let us go on . . .

From Lt-Gen R. A. Wheeler, USA, Deputy Supreme Allied Commander.

WE have beaten Germany. We are at the gates of Japan. Our job now is to finish the war in Asia.

There can be no question as to the final result. Allied courage, Allied sacrifices and Allied arms are more than equal to the task. Let us get on with it.

We can go home to a peaceful world as soon as it is done.

We'll crush Japan

From Lt-Gen Sir Oliver Leese, C-in-C, Allied Land Forces.

WITH the utter defeat of Germany, we welcome today the end of the first phase of the War.

We have watched the victorious campaign of our comrades of the BLA, under Field Marshal Montgomery, with the same pride and interest as they are watching our own progress.

This is a great day for all of us in Allied Land Forces, and for our families and friends at Home. From today onwards, we know that the full might of Great Britain and the United States—in men, ships, 'planes, guns and tanks—will be thrown in to crush Japan.

It is not possible to transport great numbers of troops and supplies to this distant theatre in a matter of weeks. But the plans to move them were made many months ago. We can be certain that not a day will be lost.

The final stages in the defeat of Japan may yet be long and hard. But our fighting men have defeated the Japanese again and again. Already they have brought us far on the road to Victory in this theatre.

I am confident that the defeat of Japan is as certain today as the defeat of Germany has been for months past.

Problems face us

From Admiral Sir Arthur Power, C-in-C, East Indies Fleet.

THE complete defeat of the German nation frees the World of a most hideous regime of oppression, crime and corruption. It opens up possibilities for mankind to live in a decent peaceful Christian manner.

The upheaval that started in 1939 will take very many years to subside and the future, while full of hope, is obscure. Nations and individuals are now faced with problems no less complex than those of recent years. Courageous and unselfish conduct in peace will alone secure our hard won victory and ultimately freedom from the threat of war.

As nations we must avoid the mistakes of 1918-1939. As individuals we must select our political leaders with care and judgment and then follow them with loyalty.

It is right to rejoice over the downfall of the Germans and the impending destruction of their bestial ally, but in so doing let us remember the sufferings of their victims and be dignified in all our actions.

Ready to expand

From Air Marshal Sir Keith Park, C-in-C, Air Command.

THIS is the first of the two great days for which we have all worked and fought for so long. Today Germany is defeated. Soon the main Allied war effort will swing from the West to the East.

As we think with deep gratitude of all those who made possible the tremendous air offensive that did so much to bring about the German defeat, all of us of Air Command, South East Asia realise the great responsibilities and traditions they are now handing on to us.

Air Command, South East Asia is ready to expand. Ever since the dark days of the 1942 retreats, the Allied Air Forces in this theatre have been preparing for this day.

Thanks to the unremitting labour and devotion to duty of all ranks our striking power has steadily grown. In January this year our aircraft made four and a half times as many sorties as in January 1944, and their bomb-loads were seven times greater.

This last February the weight of bombs dropped was almost as heavy again as the heaviest dropped in any month last year. This increase has been achieved while the main Allied effort has been concentrated in the West.

Now we can look forward to greater striking power with the whole Allied effort concentrated behind us. In closest co-operation with the Army and the Navy, Air Command will go forward in ever increasing strength to hasten the dawn of the second great day for which we fight—the defeat of Japan.

Quickest way home

From Lt-Gen Sir William Slim, Commander, Fourteenth Army.

THE war in Europe is over. The war in Asia goes on. Until that war ends too, in the unconditional surrender of a savage and brutal enemy there will be no peace in the world, nor will there be any prospect of security for our children. Towards that end no one has done more than you who have fought, flown and endured through the Burma campaigns.

Up to now because of the hard necessities of a world-wide war you have fought with meagre resources. But you have accomplished much with little. Now, to join us in the final wiping out of the evil in the East, will come the strength that has overthrown a mightier enemy in the West.

Victory, which was always certain, will now be near. How near will depend on the way in which we keep up our ruthless pressure on the shaken enemy. Let us finish the job we have so well begun. The quickest way home is the longest way round—through Tokyo.

VICTORY

By Edmund Blunden

NOW the great vision which we dared believe
Through slow and savage years is all our own;
That summit which we willed we now achieve,
And certainty deposes the unknown;
Through dragons country midnight-black we went,
Where one Apollyon had us much in mind,
And set whatever deaths he could invent,
Above, beneath, about. That lies behind.
A widening wonder glitters on our view;
That tyranny's overpast; once more we have come through.

IMMENSE the scene, the drama measureless
Which after-comers with astonished eyes
Will long survey and struggle to express,
The problem huge, the countering enterprise.
When Time makes plain the action in all parts,
Discloses things in crisis as yet hid,
Then will the world with eloquence of arts
For ever crown what these free spirits did.
We may not voice them yet, the dawn's still new,
But we live triumph now no artist ever drew.

TO trace the roads which led us to this hour
History shall be proud, and honour fill
Her halls with colours; let those bright works flower
In their due season,—we are mindful still
Of yesternight's red shadows and fierce toil,
Of this man's death and that man's master-stroke,
Of years turned ages on an alien soil,
Of fiery horrors whelming patient folk,
Of weaponcraft beyond what any knew,
Blastings, soul-witherings, hungers, eyes of death on you.

AND from the distance, from far-sundered lands,
Came men and women leaving all they had,
Into the battle fields of scorching sands,
And houseless wastes, and plains obscure and sad,
For nothing that should be a personal gain
But to ensure the best should still prevail;
The sky was flashing with their quick disdain
Of danger, under sea they would assail
The creed they counted worse than death, their crew
Swept the broad sea till nothing showed there to pursue.

THESE in their multitude and more than these,
Dying and suffering, companied, alone,
Their faces, voices, humours, tragedies,
Their will, their skill, now intimately known;
And those their leaders of one mind to frame
Vast strategies from which escape was none,
And all their actions rise to future fame;
Be theirs sweet peace, dear love, kind rain and sun,
The life for which they marched and sailed and flew,
Reunion, restoration, freedom deep and true.

BUT could our striving wishes bring us back
Those who in youth, those golden hearts and heads
Who fell untimely by the cratered track,
The vision would excel what now it sheds
Of blessing in this world; how shall we then
But by their memory rule what lies before
And from their genius light such ways that men
Through such convulsion never labour more
Thence shall the final victory ever new
Sing in the lives of all that live, "We have come through."

ANGLO GIVES YOU YOUR V-DAY SMILE

"All right, chaps. Armistice in Europe has been declared—break for five minutes' smoke."

WHY WE WON

Continued from Page Two

which they had equipped themselves. But it would also have been an impossibility but for the careful advance planning and above all the administrative planning. That I consider was one of the great achievements of the war.

The use of our means of transit, of our coastal shipping, of our railways; the concentration of the forces; the scheme for the build-up from the first extremely light fighting scale on the beaches to the full scale of equipment; the special means adopted for carrying on beach landings until we had acquired major ports, which deceived the Germans as to the rate at which we could achieve full strength in Lower Normandy—these were all masterly.

The Walls Fell

An immense amount of details had been got together, sorted out, and rearranged by the administrative planning staff into a perfect system of machinery, which has never been excelled in the history of war. It needed to be perfect, since no invasion has ever been planned or carried out in face of such long and thorough preparation to oppose it.

We should beware of thinking now, as we look back, that because the walls of Jericho fell down with such a resounding crash this meant that they were not strong or that it was an easy matter to overthrow them. They were very strong indeed. It was only because we had made such thorough preparation to deal them an overwhelming blow that they fell.

And that blow was dealt by armies standing in what has always been recognised as a weak and perilous position holding a narrow foothold ashore after a landing in face of opposition.

I have less need to emphasise the brilliance of the plan by which the German armies in Normandy were defeated because that is so recent in everyone's mind and has been so thoroughly discussed. The great pincer movement between Falaise and Argentan was a masterpiece and we shall always take pride that it was one of our own commanders, Field-Marshal Montgomery, who conceived and timed it. The Germans were led on to contribute to their own disaster. I believe I am right in saying that even their counter-offensive towards Avranches, which sealed their fate, was in a broad sense foreseen.

But victory on the battlefield is rarely decisive without exploitation and pursuit, and countless great victories in history have remained relatively barren because it has been found impossible to organise an exploitation worthy of them.

Like A Rabble

Here the exploitation was of the same standard as the victory on the battlefield. The Germans were run off their feet. Their vehicles were destroyed by tens of thousands from the air. Huge pockets were cut off all over the country. It was in those days the last few days of August, the first part of September that the German armies in the West were finally reduced to a rabble and that the way was made ready for the last blows against Germany.

I have spoken only of the strictly military side, saying nothing about organisation of man-power, of capital, of material; about propaganda, ship-repair, and many other vital subjects which contributed to victory. But perhaps I have indicated as well as I can manage to do it in so short a space some of the main reasons why we survived and won. If I had to give a master-reason I should say, in four words, it was command of the sea.

"I, WALTER BAYNE"

At zero-hour we go forward—
Now, while the crickets' song is
yet about my ears,
And the darkness before dawn
wraps me in a shroud of
thoughts,
I, Walter Bayne, thank God
Almighty
For the blessing of a true friend.

There was a day when the
doubting clouds of youth
Were scattered by a ray of
radiant light,
When first I looked deep into the
depths of blue eyes,
When first my soul took flight
from its own imprisonment
And joined hands in budding
fullness with the soul of her
I loved.
Before the last blossom of spring
had burst its bonds
Our lives were one.

Summer was ours; the thrush
sang for us,
Moonlight-dappled waters lap-
ping, lapping,
Echoed our whispered intimacies.
We entwined our limbs in shady
woods, we mingled lips by
the moon;
Till summer was gone.
Autumn brought sleep and golden
glory
But with the tatters of ripened
leaves upon the earth,
England called her sons to the
banner,
And my shoulder was wet with
tears. . . .

Now the barrage is blasting
those hilltop bunkers
Soon it will creep, and we
shall go forward.
I have courage, for God and
my wife are with me.

D. S. C.

Seac: V.E. insert of May 1945.

of, say, 17 Div? One fully appreciates the mental torture of being without news of home, etc, but what about the average Infantryman who fought his way from Dimapur to Mandalay or Rangoon? Is he now to be pushed aside in this wave of mass sentiment? The average P.O.W. looks apparently a great deal fitter than the man who has fought his way for 1,000 miles over the most difficult terrain, in the worst climatic conditions.

This is not a matter of 'sour grapes'; we are all non-Infanteers. It is just the view of a bunch of onlookers who have seen what the other fellow has had to go through.

From Tpr. J. Holbrook, Recce Regt. R.A.C.:

Here is my Grand Repatriation Scheme. All men due for repat. should march home. On the way back we should live on de-hydrated yak's milk and little button-quail. Marco Polo did it. Why can't we?

How about the English Channel? I calculate that when we reach Calais the Channel Tunnel will be completed and our triumphant march will continue unhindered.

Of course, a few malcontents will insist on going back by sea. These I propose to send home in U-boats from Lorient and Brest, the whole journey to be made under water and the temperature gradually lowered en route to re-accustom the voyagers to British mean temps. and anti-cyclones.

The following is the order in which the various categories would be sent home:

1. All ranks who have not seen their great-grandchildren for 13 years.

2. All ranks who promise to go home and have 15 children in $16\frac{1}{2}$ years. (They also receive the '39–'43 Star).

3. All single ranks who have had their 'bottom-drawers' broken-up since going overseas.

4. All ranks who have had malaria 55 times.

5. All ranks who have been through two monsoons without a monsoon cape.

6. All ranks who don't want to stop here.

From Australian Pte. C. Brown writing from Thailand:

With wrath we of this camp learned this morning of a new order to the effect that ex-P.O.W.s must salute all Japanese officers.

No one who has not witnessed the countless humiliations and cruelties inflicted on P.O.W.s by the Japanese can appreciate the anger and disgust that this order excites in us.

For more than three years these simian sadists have insisted that all P.O.W.s (from colonel to private) salute *all* members of the Jap Army.

We Australians suspect the order emanates from one of the

79

not-yet-extinct Poona pukka sahib type, the type that sees something sacrosanct in an officer – any officer.

We salute our own officers because they hold the King's commission. But we Australians absolutely refuse to pay the same compliment to the holders of commissions granted by that moth-eaten deity Hirohito.

From R. James:

Do we want sponsored radio? My answer to that one is a very emphatic 'no'. Let me make it clear however, that I am not upholding the B.B.C. as the perfect model for broadcasting. Most of their stuff is deadly dull and as for their variety – better acts have been chased out of fourth rate music halls.

But I do object to sponsored radio on the following grounds:

Such broadcasting is primarily a form of advertising and therefore must be designed to catch the ear of the public as a whole – a public notoriously depraved in taste. The result would be that the stuff broadcast would reach a new low in banality, monotony and sheer bad taste. Mark you, I do not object to hearing some good music by the courtesy of Nit Wits Chewing Gum Incorporated – but what I do object to is the fact that we would hear ad nauseam 'Boo Hoo Hoo I Love You' sponsored by Liquorice Lip Stick (Makes your kisses taste sweeter and last longer).

That is the kind of thing which big business think the public wants (and they are not so far wrong at that) and this is the kind of thing we would get. It would be goodbye to sanity and intelligence for in the morning we would be assailed by the *Daily Express* and the *Daily Mirror* – biggest and best because they shout loudest – and in the evening by sugary sentiment designed to persuade us that when we did turn the damn thing off we should clean our teeth with 'Shino' and have better dreams on a Maudlin Mattress.

No. Let us have the B.B.C. with all its faults. Because the B.B.C. is quite disinterested in advertising and enjoys financial freedom, the people who run it can afford to give us intelligent talks, good music, and let us hear the views of people who have got something to say; they are not at the mercy of financiers who scream 'sell my soap and hang the public taste; I don't care whether or not you destroy it.'

In other words the B.B.C. can live by the dictum of giving the public what is good for it in the form in which it likes it – a dictum which sponsored radio cannot accept. And it's a truth and a responsibility which has been forgotten by the daily Press. We should not allow it to be buried in its last ditch.

From 'Shorty' in Ceylon:

I arst you 'ow is it after all these years they've suddenly taken it

Service Copy

VICTORY

Vol. II

No. 11

4 AS.

Sun-dressed cover girls to remind men in the
front line of the green lawns
of their homeland.

Disquiet on the Eastern front, as Hitler, Mussolini, Keitel and
Jodl study a map of the campaign. Russian successes changed the anti-Communist
fears of Britain and her allies into enthusiastic
support for Stalin. *Signal*.

into their 'eds that we musn't show our you-and-me's no more? 'Ow is it they never make up their minds, if they've got any? Like when we come out 'ere in them Wolsey topees what ought to 'ave been made of china that's all they're good for – and soon as we land they takes 'em off of us I suppose to send 'em back for the next batch comin' out 'ere to keep their 'eds warm on the boat.

Same with them barmy shorts wot we 'ad to turn down and tuck in our 'ose tops. In our mob we arst the Q. bloke if we could 'ave a pair cut down for daytimes but 'e seys no we're 'andin 'em in and 'avin slacks instead. Can you beat it? There must be an 'ell of a pile of junk somewhere of the stuff they gives you in Blighty and takes off of you out 'ere.

'Mozzies' from *Seac*.

And now the 'ot season's 'ere we're going to sweat much better round the knees just because some brass 'at aint got 'em brown yet I suppose and don't want no one to see 'em. Or is it because of mozzies, because if so I suppose the W.A.A.F.s and R.A.F. and W.R.E.N.s don't get bit much? Wouldn't surprise me if they told 'em to wear their nighties – not the R.A.F. – the W.A.A.F.s and W.R.E.N.s I mean. I suppose the R.A.F. don't bother about mozzies they're always up in the air theirselves anyway. Another thing, funny 'ow mozzies like your knees and not your elbows. I suppose in the daytime it's a special kind of knee-mosquito. Not 'arf. Like at a certain cinema I know 'ere, where they've got a smashin' king what bites anywhere through anything.

Anyway, me and my mates don't know where we stand so I done the enclosed drorins and we'd be much obliged if you'd inform us as to just what we 'ave got to wear.

From 'Y':

If an explanation can be supplied which will satisfy all the services regarding the following point a lot of bad feeling will be allayed.

HOW TO USE ANTI·MOSQUITO CREAM!

THE REDOUBTABLE PROF PHLITT TACKLES THE STICKY PROBLEM OF INSECT REPELLANTS

Anti-mosquito cream should not be confused with Auntie Mabel or Auntie Florence, who are two of the nicest people living. Anti-mosquito cream is a thick, opaque substance which makes a dandy lubricant for greasing the back axles of squeaky prams, a nifty hair pomade, and is also an indispensable household dressing for sun-burn, chapped hands, dhobi itch and Bengal rot. As a last resource it can be used to alleviate the skeeter menace.

I claim no patent for my method, but directions must be followed with the greatest of care for the best results.

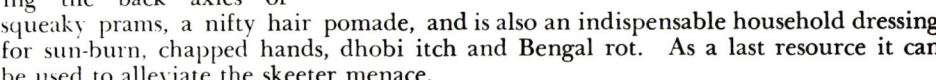

The deadly anti-mosquito weapon from *Seac*.

FIG I. Prop open a tin of anti-mosquito cream with a match to which a length of cotton is attached. Now it's just a question of waiting.

FIG. II. Goody! Here comes the little pest, rootin' around for trouble. Watch your step, Albert this place is dynamite!

FIG. III. Tch! Tch! And as if you weren't warned too! Well all I can say is you boys will have to learn the hard way!

At a recent free E N S A show the first four or five rows of seats were reserved for officers. This sort of occurrence is frequent and E N S A are blamed for such being their policy. It seems more likely, however, that the officials who arrange the accommodation for the show are at fault.

Apparent class distinction of this nature is not what we are fighting for.

Editor's reply:

E N S A provides the concert parties and stars; the allocation of seats is made by an inter-services committee and in the case of a show at a unit the seating is at the discretion of the C.O. It is E N S A policy that the front seats be divided, half for other ranks and half for officers, and when the seating arrangements are not in ENSA's hands a recommendation is made to that effect. When the seating is in ENSA's hands, that policy is strictly adhered to. In the case of shows at the R.A.F. Theatre only ten per cent of the tickets have been allocated to officers.

From a few airmen in S.E.A.A.F.:

We have just returned from seeing an ENSA show in Akyab. We were disgusted, not with the show, but with the audience – or rather a minority of the audience whose rowdyism ruined everyone else's enjoyment.

The show was enjoyable until a bunch of vulgar rowdies began to exercise their 'wit' in indecencies which made us blush for the feelings of the girls who had travelled out to this part of the world to provide our entertainment. They must have been most embarrassed.

Never before have we been so ashamed of our countrymen. Is this the British spirit of fair play and decency, or consideration for others?

We would like the ENSA company to realise that most of us enjoyed *Variety Vanities*, and would ask them to accept our apologies for the conduct of our fellow-servicemen who could not behave properly.

Rhyme and Line

Thousands of civilians had entered the army several months before the outbreak of war as militia men, and right from the 'off', with more and more men being called up for the forces, poets and artists who were caught up in an unfamiliar and inhibiting way of life sought self-expression in the pages of service publications which seemed to encourage their efforts. As servicemen were posted far and wide and the number of service publications grew, artists and writers strove to spotlight every facet of service life, often with devastating effect.

Battle Dress, the cadet magazine for embryo officers, published in February 1940, contained a good many poems by cadets as well as a book review devoted mainly to the poetry of A. E. Housman. It seemed that the stage was being set for the emergence of officer poets who would attain the stature of First World War poets such as Siegfried Sassoon, Robert Nichols, or William Noel Hodgson. A twenty-seven-year-old professor training to be an officer, Enoch Powell, contributed a short poem, 'Last Love', in which an incipient sourness could be detected.

A poem by an editor of the magazine, Alan Crick, M.A., Ph.D., who had been the vice-consul at Danzig in 1938–9, was called 'Ignorance' and may have been inspired by 'The Walrus and the Carpenter':

> The law of gravity holds good,
> Though never really understood,
> And everyone who lives must die,
> Yet no one knows the reason why.
>
> Or why the whole is such a size
> And crabs are unlike butterflies,
> Or how it is that men wear spats,
> Wigs, monocles, and bowler hats.
>
> I know of none who can explain
> Just why a drain is called a drain,
> A jug a jug, a pin a pin,
> And why polygamy is sin.

"And of course, you can forget all that stuff you used to read in the 'Boys Magazine' about lions and things . . ."

From *Jambo*.

And why it is that blue-black ink
Is hardly ever good to drink,
You see, one's ignorance is such
We really don't know very much.

A poem by R.H.B., who could possibly have been a padre trying to loosen his dog-collar, threw in a bit of religion for the magazine, just to show it was not composed entirely of laboured frivolity, reflected culture, literary aspirations, and tailors' advertisements. His poem was entitled '1940':

High on a hill against a sullen sky
The Lord of Heav'n was left to groan and die,
He died to redeem from sin
The sons of men who never heeded H I M.

Two thousand years have gone. Now who must pay
To ransom men from slavery?
The simple soldier for our common weal
Lies dying on a cross of steel.

As the war dragged on, poets popped up in service publications in every theatre of war. *Union Jack, Contact, Victory, Jambo,* and American publications such as *Stars and Stripes, C.B.I. Roundup,* and *Yank,* invariably carried a small quota of offerings from service poets as well as poems by such well-known poets as A. E. Housman, Edmund Blunden, V. Sackville-West, and Lord Dunsany. According to an article by Gordon Waterfield published in London and reprinted in *Seac* in March 1945, poetry had an especial appeal in wartime and many books of poems were being published in London.

Typically American are these poems which appeared in *Stars and Stripes* in May 1942:

85

Dear Mom. Although I'm far away,
You're in my thoughts this very day;
I see the smile upon your face,
The one that brightens every place,
And Mom, although I am not so much,
Your teachings always have been such,
That I am sure I'll be O.K.
So don't you fret about what folks say.
When things are tough, it's good to know
Your prayers can follow where I go
And though I've never told before
It's you, dear Mom, that I adore.
My only wish in life today
Will come true when I hear you say
'I'm proud of you as I can be'
Yes that is praise enough for me.

Army Cartoons

Cartoons from service contributions to *Yank*.

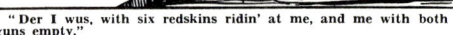

"Der I wus, with six redskins ridin' at me, and me with both guns empty."

"It was an Irish girl I met in the blackout!"

No doubt about it, the poet, James C. Hayes, was proud of his Mom,
but no prouder than the poet who diffidently signed himself E.M.L.
and wrote this poem worthy of a place on any greetings card:

In dreams I dream I always see
A face that is most dear to me.
Though far away it seems so near;
Each feature is so soft and clear.
No Whistler could with brush and paint
Picture the beauty of this Saint,
As to my mind her face appears
Through all the days in all the years.
My Mother is my faithful friend
I know she'll be that to the end.

She gave to me her loving care
Abundantly, with much to spare.

Capt. Thompson Rich came up with a song for V-Day. Published in *Roundup* in April 1945, a month before the end of the war, it was called 'Der Tag':

The Nazis are flying, the Nazis are flying . . .
Red in the west their sun goes down,
Flat on their breasts their ranks are lying,
Flat on their breasts they bleed and drown.

The Nazis are dying, the Nazis are dying . . .
Their flags are furled, their warriors sleep,
Over the world their women are crying,
Over the world their unborn weep.

Over the world new hope is making,
Over the world new dawn is breaking
Driving the murderous night to rout,
Over the world new day is waking . . .
Over the world a prayer goes out.

In the same issue of *Roundup* was the poem 'The American Red Cross' by Pvt. Rastus Corley, a member of a Negro A.A.A. battery in Myitkyana, Burma, which appeared under the headline 'Prolific Poet Rastus Crashes Roundup'. It seems that the indomitable Rastus had previously submitted more than two hundred poems produced during twenty-one months in the India-Burma theatre of war, without any success, and that for his 'eagerness, dogged endurance and fine spirit' he was being rewarded by seeing his work in print. Corley's poem scored more points than 'Der Tag' for expressing a sentiment straight from the heart:

In the States to me it was just a name.
The way they asked for money, I thought it was a shame,
From now on I won't be like that anymore,
Because the money we give, I know what it's for.
They give us cigarettes and all kinds of stuff.
And I believe the money we give isn't half enough.
They do all this to keep you from feeling blue,
And all the money you give, they give right back to you.
God bless the American Red Cross!
They are helping to keep our soul from being lost.
They are keeping us happy and are too good to me.
Because everything they give us is absolutely free.

The Desert Army magazine, *The Crusader*, featured army poets in 'Poets' Parade' from time to time and ran competitions for poetry. L/Cpl. L. Cerner had this poem published in February 1943 as a competition entry:

The yellow light
Like midnight candles
Fast is dripping
Weary of the fight,
Now the anxious rattle
From the gun is tapping.
Murmur of a distant motor
All the sweeter.
Like a drug, beginning to seep
Delicious silence, bring with it sleep.

[By Sergeant D. Davies.

And as they used to say at Aldershot :—

From *Battle Dress*, 1940.

In lighter vein, but a cry from the heart nevertheless, was 'The Dentist's Lament' by Capt. L. B. Weeks, Army Dental Corps, which appeared in *Jambo* in February 1944:

To a Provincial Englishman a painful Dentist, too,
Sailing halfway round the world is a wonderous thing to
    do.
The Gleam of Flying fishes and tang of ocean foam,
Is distant far from 'open wide' and the stodginess of home.

To 'Pull' and 'Fill' and 'Scrape' and 'Clean' I came 10,000
    miles,
Past Cancer and past Capricorn with Durban's winning wiles,
Into a strange and tropic land across a vasty plain,
Nairobi for a week or two and off to sea again.

To 'Pull' and 'Fill' and 'Scrape' and 'Clean' has filled each
    waking hour,
From Addis down to Berbera, Harrar to Dire-Dana
On mountain top I've yanked the tooth and wielded a fearful
    drill,
On sweltering plain I've cured the pain, of heat I've had
    my fill.

88

But whether in smallish English town where the cold Nor'
      Easter bites,
Or weltering wet in Berbera sweat 'neath glinting tropic lights,
The fact remains in every clime, with every colour and race,
They hate to come and visit me, I see it in every face.

Cartoon by Sgt. Ralph Stein
from *Yank*.

"When the chips are down a man starts thinkin' about his family."

A vet also had his say. 'Conscience Balm' was written by Maj. Harry
Hobbs, V.D., whilst serving in South-East Asia in 1944:

The horse and mule live thirty years,
And nothing know of wine and beers.
The goat and sheep at twenty die,
And never taste of Scotch or Rye.
The cow drinks water by the ton,
At eighteen she is nearly done.
The dog at fifteen cashes in,
Without the aid of rum and gin.
The cat in milk and water soaks,
And then in twelve short years it croaks,
The modest, sober, bone-dry hen,
Lays eggs for noggs, then dies at ten.
All animals are strictly dry,
They sinless live and swiftly die.
But sinful, ginful, horsy men
Survive for three-score years and ten!

Poets and artists serving in South-East Asia found plenty of scope
for expression in *Seac*, which featured poems and cartoons practically
every day. Humorous or serious, often crude, these always had something pertinent to say and more often than not scored a bull's-eye
with the boys. The Home Front, the pestiferous mosquito, the mystery
sausage known as the 'soya link', 'bully beef', 'gongs', the Establishment, 'bull', the local scene and customs, were all harpooned,

lampooned, and cartooned. Sentimental reminiscences and home thoughts were expressed in rhyme and line. Not a trick was missed. Every theatre of war, every unit had its own peculiar jargon and background, but generally army jargon was universal, with British army adaptations of Urdu, Arabic, Kiswahili, and a wealth of expressive swear words, thrown in for good measure.

"I promised my mother not to get my feet wet."

Soldier.

Frank Owen, perhaps the most famous of service editors, wrote in his Foreword to *Laugh with Seac*:

> The men 'up there' drew their own cartoons, wrote their own jingles and bunged 'em back to their own paper, *Seac*. They arrived in odd shapes and forms scribbled on the backs of service forms with stubs of pencils as they occurred to men on gunsites or in foxholes or on airstrips. We gave the artists and poets ten rupees a time and they gave half a million of their comrades a good belly laugh. I think few newspapers ever made a better bargain.

Jack Bridges, serving with the R.A.F. on a forward airstrip up in the Arakan, had many cartoons published in *Seac* and *Victory* under the pseudonym of Feste (from Shakespeare's character in *Twelfth Night*). Bridges had a dry sense of humour and his drawings were slick. On the other hand wags such as 'Tock' Williams and 'Wild Bill' Hickman, both of Commando S.B.S., who had good ideas but could not draw for toffee, relied on a comrade who could draw to translate their jokes into line drawings. Among the many other cartoonists popular in South-East Asia were Britons Nicolson, Jacey, Fisher, Cott, Gwil, and Frolik, and Americans Ehret, Somerville, and Ted Satley.

Frolik, a prolific and clever cartoonist, wrote many humorous

90

poems and skits on a variety of subjects pertinent to troops serving in India and Burma, where a bed was a 'charpoy' and 'charpoy bashing' was taking a nap, where tea was 'char' and everyone was some 'wallah' or other, and a 'basha' was a bug-infested hut made of palm fronds which served as home to servicemen lucky to have a roof over their heads. Frolik's humour is illustrated by the following poems from *Seac* which were reprinted in *Laugh with Seac* in 1946:

MORE IF

If you can do your three and eight unbroken
Yet find your views on life are just the same;
If you can still speak English as it's spoken,
And still give tea its good old-fashioned name;

If you can laugh at mud above your ankles
Or grin at dust that burns within your throat;
If you don't grouse at everything that rankles;
Nor dream too much of rolling on that boat;

If you can eat and not grow tired of eating
The stuff that comes in tins from Argentine;
If you've no inner voice that keeps repeating
'I will not, dare not, face another bean!'
If you feel cheesed yet somehow keep your chin up
And make a tiny molehill of your cares;
If you can gaze upon a Varga pin-up
Yet keep your thoughts from running up them stairs;

If you were there and do not talk about it
When you are told to get some service in,
You are, and there is none who'll dare to doubt it,
A better man than I am, Gunga Din!

JUNGLE SCENE

Down in the jungle something stirred,
It might be a Jap or it might be a bird.
I cock up my rifle and silently creep
Into the undergrowth thick and deep.

I come to a clearing and suddenly see
Tiny bells swinging from every tree
Bluebells and buttercups on the ground
With fairy folk dancing all around.

I pinch my arm and I rub my eyes
O hark to the joyful fairy cries?
Mark how the foxgloves gently sway
To join with the fairies in their play!

I put up my rifle and quietly withdraw
And a gruff voice asks me what I saw,
'Fairies, dear Sergeant' I make reply
And that's how I got 7 days R.I.

But Frolik could be deadly serious, as in 'Trial by Fury', first published in *Seac* in May 1945:

'Shoot all the menfolk!' the Daily Blah cries,
'Put all their women in fetters!
'Teach all their children a new set of lies,
'Teach 'em respect for their betters!'

Careful, my countrymen, guard what you say,
Think twice as you reach for your guns,
Lest history ask in its pertinent way
'I wonder which crowd were the Huns?'

Many serious poets did not confine their thoughts to their own theatres of war and sought inspiration in wider fields and issues, sometimes exploring ethical and spiritual areas. In September 1944, W. B. in *Seac* rounded on Rumania in a scathing attack on Germany's satellites. His poem was simply called 'Rumania':

Judas kissed Christ. So now through the ages
Is he synonymous with lies and mire.
Now any swine who voids on history's pages
Only to second place can he aspire.
Poor Teuton satellites, you nothing gain
By rolling Ananias into Cain;
Even the Crown of Infamy you miss
Thwarted from that and merely by a kiss.

James A. Mackereth's 'Eternal Moment' was a crystal thought glittering in dark times:

The ever-living moment passes soon
To twinkle in the darkness like a star,
To come again for ever, bane or boon,
A foreigner from far.
Most mighty pinions touch us as they pass
With rhythmic indulations round the spheres.
The splendid prides of time like splintered glass
Fall through our vision from ten thousand years.
And all our knowledge knows, history tells,
Is a twinkling in the mind of elfin bells.

P. J. Martin provided a clean, crisp, refreshing note for the hot and the homesick with his 'Nanda Devi' in March 1945:

Down below,
    The lake glistened
In the fresh morning sun

92

'No! no! I'm N O T Grey
Wolf!' Cartoon by Feste from
Seac.

And the man not looking, listened
To the uneven run
   Of shrill notes in the pines.

Far below,
   The earth shifted
On the dry, hazy heat
   And the dreary rivers drifted
On the flat yellow sheet
   Of dust, down through the plains.

But the man
   Stood, leaf shaded,
With his brown eyes bright
   And all other things faded
In the sheer crystal light
   Of snows far away.

93

Michael Storm's 'Professor Phlitt' from *Seac*.

'Monsoon Sortie' by 'Groupie', published in *Seac* in September 1945, was a rasping and evocative poem, a reminder of the part being played by the air forces in South-East Asia:

Near dawn an engine's clamour shatters sleep,
Elusive hard-gained sleep, the only balm
For mind distorted by the ceaseless psalm
of hissing rain . . . Roar stops
    Into the deep
Monotony of foetid wetness seep

Our sodden souls. Lethargic, listless palm
Drips in the dark grey gloom, the airless calm
Of dawn. No wind, no motion, save the weep
From shapeless drifts of murky wrack; and now
Their torturing of Mother Earth – with beat of pattering rain,
Splashing upon her sweltering fevered brow –
Enforce their torrid rape with humid heat
To whelp the slimy growths of rolling rain.

Another sharply descriptive poem, about Burma, was 'Kabaw Valley' by E.D.C.P., published in *Seac* in October 1945:

Yes, I have known Tamu.
Who could forget
That narrow road winding sharply down
Into the stifling foetid valley;
Deeper, ever deeper,
Through dark dripping trees
Down to the red swirling river
Swollen with heavy monsoon rain?
Pelting, stinging rain, sweeping down the valley.

Who could forget
The humid steaming heat
And myriad little mango flies
Hovering tormentingly around one's eyes,
The woodpeckers' strange shrill call
Falling suddenly
From the high summit of a teak tree?

Who could forget
The great molten moon
Illuminating with fantastic beauty
The dark jungle,
The tue-toos' tired call,
The bull frogs' raucous croaking
From the depths of a dark monsoon ditch,
Shattering the still night?

Who could forget Tamu?
And yet how long will you remember?
For even now the jungle claims her own
And covers empty camping grounds,
Ugly twisted steel,
Charred wood and battle scars
With tall green grass and winding tendrils –
Heedless of those gone on:
A shelter for the dead who lie at rest in
her green solitude
Amid the music of the strange cicadas' call
And wild birds' haunting cry.

K. C. Baxter's 'Sonnet for Anne', which appeared in *Seac* on 23 October 1945, a few months after the Japanese surrender, struck a poignant note after the 'tumult and shouting' had died away:

Your quiet presence consecrates the air,
    And benediction follows in your wake;
Beauty attends you and for your dear sake
    Our woods renew themselves, our meadows wear,
As for a bridal, flowers in their hair.
    Not but for you the hazel-tree doth shake
Her yellow tassels loosely o'er the lake,
    Nor but for you the birds sing everywhere.

Then stay, then stay, and leave me not again
    To mourn as one bereaved your going hence,
As one bereaved to recollect – in vain,
    Sweet, your most loved and lovely influence:
Persephone from fields of asphodel
    Was snatched away – and will you go as well?

Anglo, who, like Frolik, turned in many cartoons for *Seac*, also tried his hand at writing poetry, but unlike Frolik he always tried a more serious approach as a change from endeavouring to be

Anglo cartoon from *Seac*.

" Alright chaps,—Armistice in Europe has been declared—break for five minutes smoke! "

The Camel Corps comes home, to the amazement of the customers of the
White Swan and village locals; *Parade* was distributed throughout
the North African and Middle Eastern
battle areas.

This impression forms the lively and bright cover of a Japanese service
newspaper. The wrenching of troops from their homes,
and their movement to foreign lands, aroused
many new responses which found expression
in painting and poetry.

humourous in his cartoons. *Seac* published many of his poems, some of which appeared in *The Statesmen* and *The Straits Times*, for which he also drew cartoons. Other publications which published his work included *Roundup*, *Free Press*, *Singapore*, and *Soldier* in Europe. Three of his poems follow:

THROUGH ETHER

I am not here:
   Though I walk in the heat of day,
And rest through the dark hours of night,
   I am not here
But a thousand miles away.
   Though I breathe and eat and sleep,
And see and act and speak,
   There is no cheer;
I am not here.
   A disassociated self
The ether spans,
   And lives the life the body bans:
Though I am, I am not:
   It is clear,
I am not here.

TROOPSHIP TO INDIA

The sun slides down beneath the waves
   And pinkly tints the frothing foam;
Smoky shadows are gliding past
   Slowly across the blood red dome.
And pensive standing at the rail
   Watching even as day departs,
I know each shadow bears a host;
   Bodies receding from their hearts.

PHILOSOPHER'S STONE

Values change as the years pass:
   What is exclusive one year
The next year is for the mass.
   Gold will be of less value than brass
When there is freedom from want and fear;
   And what the alchemist sought in yesteryear,
Will one day come to pass,
   When the Philosopher's stone is found,
Not buried underground
   But where placed by Rodin,
Symbolically discreet,
   It serves as a resting place
For his 'Thinker's' seat.

On the subject of cartoons the editorial column in *Sunday Seac* on 4 March 1945 had this to say:

> The humorous artist, the cartoonist and the creator of comic strips are doing nearly as much as the film star and the band leader to relieve the war of some of its loneliness. The cartoonist, indeed, is helping to win it.

A pointed political comment from David Low, a humorous drawing from one of our own South East Asia artists such as Frolik or Anglo or Michael Storm, or the adventures of Jane and Jake liquidate that browned-off feeling.

Jon's famous 'Two types' from *Union Jack*.

" Got the right idea old boy "

Jon's fabulous 'Two types' must still be remembered by thousands the world over. Brian Robb, cartoonist and illustrator in *The Crusader*, was well known at home and abroad; and Edgar Legnan's 'Crusader Cutie' was a popular pin-up. Peter Ender and Friell appeared in *Soldier*, the army magazine that is still running today. Everyone in East Africa knew Finch, Speirs, and Jet. Among American cartoonists, Bill Mauldin, whose bearded foxhole-dwelling G.I. in the series 'Up Front' enjoyed a popularity far beyond the pages of *Stars and Stripes*, was awarded a Pulitzer Prize for one of his cartoons. Cpl. Dave Breger's 'Sad Sack' in *Yank* had a huge service following which followed him into the lucrative field of syndicated publication in civvy street.

'And what do you think this
is – a birthmark?' Jon cartoon
from *Union Jack*.

English and American national newspapers donated cartoons and
strips to service publications. Jane from the *Daily Mirror* appeared
in various stages of undress in *Union Jack* and *Seac* and even in *C.B.I.
Roundup*. Popeye popped up in *Union Jack*, and Superman, Li'l Abner,
Joe Palooka, and Blondie were featured at some time or other in *Stars
and Stripes*. Bruce Bairnsfather, the veteran World War I cartoonist,
drew a regular cartoon in *Stars and Stripes* in 1942. *Punch* cartoonist
David Langdon and Giles of the *Express* were often featured in service
publications, as were Pat Auld, Hynes, and Fenwicke, contributors
to *Lilliput*, *Men Only*, and *London Opinion*.

Dozens of service artists had their work published in widely
circulated service publications such as *Parade*, *Victory*, *Seac*, and *The
Crusader*; dozens more were featured in unit and specialist publications
such as *Battle Dress* and the American *Cavalry Journal*. Perhaps now,
years later, it is hard to recapture the essence of a wartime cartoon.
Cartoons are of the moment, and when all is said and done poetry
may prove to be more lastingly evocative.

At the end of 1945, Maj. P. R. H. Molloy wrote to *Seac*:

Some day your excellent little paper will come to an end,
when South-East Asia winds up, and your readers disperse to

99

«My batman gives me two akkers a day to save himself the trouble.»

Pat Auld of *Lilliput* magazine contributed this cartoon to *Union Jack*.

the four corners of the world from which they came. To me the spirit of *Seac* was embodied in the little poems it frequently contained. These summed up in turn the feelings of sadness, frustration, fortitude and fun that all of us in this command have gone through at one time or another. Would it be possible for you to collect the best of those little poems and publish them in one volume? I am sure there are many other campaigners in S.E.A.C. who like myself would like to have a collection of these poems to browse through occasionally in the days of peace ahead to feel again emotions that undoubtedly strengthened the soul and brought a little wisdom.

In 1946, *Laugh with Seac*, a book of cartoons and humorous poems reprinted from *Seac*, was published by Frank Owen for the Supreme

Allied Commander, South-East Asia, and printed in Calcutta. Thousands of copies were sold in Britain and America as well as to servicemen still serving in South-East Asia. The following poems selected from its pages reflect the flavour of the times:

IN A BASHA

I live in a basha,
   My word it's a smasher –
Just a few old bamboo poles
   And a roof full of holes
Strung together in style
   That makes anyone smile.
When the wind comes, it shakes –
   Sometimes it just breaks.
When it rains cats and dogs
   Then it just waterlogs.
When it falls in a heap
   We're still all asleep.
For we know, after strife
   Comes a happier life.

X.Y.Z.

A COOK'S THOUGHTS ON BULLY

You can stew it, you can fry it
But no matter how you try it
Fundamentally it remains the same,
You can hash it, you can slash it,
With potatoes you can mash it
But when all is done you've only changed the name.
With some onions you can mix it,
But no matter how you fix it,
You receive no thanks but only just a yell.
In shepherd's pie you'll hide it,
But before long they'll have spied it,
Yes, they'll track it down and create merry hell.
Just a little tin of bully,
Not appreciated fully,
Just a little inoffensive sort of tin.
Yet for all your foolish pranks
It's detested in the ranks.
Therefore camouflage it well, to save your skin.

Sgt. R. Bradley

STREET SCENE

Ears cry for deafness as, from shuffling, dhotied forms
Which thread the living pattern of the garbage-littered street,
Expectorations, base and treble cleffed,
Grate and vibrate till eardrums cry 'defeat'.

Eyes cry for blindness as the strawberry-coloured streams
Of betel nut saliva drown all pity,
Weaving their obscene tapestry of filth
Over the face of the Empire's Second City.

Minds cry for madness as the throaty chorus rises,
Turning sane men to thoughts of killings;
Would that we were 'neath England's safe, smug law again . . .
'Spitting Prohibited – Fine Forty Shillings.'

Patrick Bacon

STICKING IT OUT IN DELHI

Fighting the Nazis from Delhi,
Fighting the Japs from Kashmir,
Exiled from England, we feel you should know
The way that we're taking it here.

Sticking it out at the Cecil,
Doing our bit for the war,
Going through hell
At Maiden's Hotel,
Where they stop serving lunch after four!
Sticking it out at the Cecil
For the sake of the land we adore –
But never you worry, though continents shake,
Whatever befall, our morale will not break,
Provided that Wenger's don't run out of steak –
Doing our bit for the war.

Tightening our belts at Nirula's,
Taking it all on the chin;
For the sake of the nation
We suffer privation,
Just look at the shortage of gin!
We frequently feel that in England,
They don't know the straits that we're in;
The way that we've cried at the newsreels we've seen.
(They bring it so near, if you know what we mean).
And only eight bearers instead of sixteen,
Taking it all on the chin.

Roughing it at the Imperial,
Proving we're sound to the core,
We take B.O.R.'s
For rides in our cars,

UNION ⚹ JACK

No. 1 Tuesday, June 13, 1944 Two Lire

FOR THE BRITISH FIGHTING FORCES

STOP PRESS

IT WAS OFFICIALLY REVEALED AT SUPREME HEADQUARTERS LAST NIGHT THAT THE THIRD BRITISH INFANTRY DIVISION IS IN ACTION IN NORMANDY.

BRIDGEHEAD FORCE 18 MILES IN

Pope leaves the Vatican

FOR the first time since the Germans took over Rome, the Pope left the Vatican City on Sunday.

He motored to the Basilica of Saint Ignatius, where he returned thanks for the sparing of Rome from the destruction of war.

His Holiness was absent from the Vatican for nearly an hour.

He delivered a short sermon from the pulpit of the Jesuit cathedral and conducted a service before the statue of the Virgin of the Divine Love, which is normally kept at Castelli di Leva, a few miles from Rome, but was brought into the city for protection during the war.

Meanwhile, in London, the Archbishop of Westminster (Dr. Bernard Griffin) was also giving thanks for the liberation of Rome. He paid tribute to all Allied soldiers who, by their efforts, had brought freedom to the Eternal City.

de Gaulle may visit F.D.R.

General de Gaulle has welcomed President Roosevelt's invitation to visit Washington, says Reuter's Diplomatic correspondent. But well-informed quarters believe he considers it necessary to consult the French Committee of Liberation and secure their collective support.

"UNION JACK" Central Italy Edition

The Central Italy Edition of "Union Jack" will serve areas farther forward than those formerly supplied by the Western Italy Edition.

Units interested should write, stating their requirements, to Administration Officer, "Union Jack," Central Italy Edition, "B" British Army Newspaper Unit, C.M.F.

ALTHOUGH German resistance has grown more desperate, further progress has been made by the Allied forces in France and the bridgehead is now regarded as being practically secure.

Late last night it was reported that the bridgehead had been widened to 65 miles and that the Allies were 18 miles inland at the deepest point.

Fierce tank battles are still raging, say messages from Supreme Allied Headquarters, in the Caen area, where Rommel's 21st and 12th Panzer Divisions are being reinforced in their attempt to stem the British and Canadian armour, now threatening to outflank this key centre.

German reports that Carentan, the important road junction in the centre area, had fallen were unconfirmed until the evening, when Reuter messages spoke of an important gain by U.S. troops who had fought through a flooded area to capture the town. Grim fighting had taken place in marsh and deep water.

In the central sector, further advances have taken place following the capture of Trevieres, which lies west of Bayeux.

Correspondents with the American forces concerned, say Trevieres is now a heap of rubble. The town fell at dawn after a night-long battle in which the bayonet and grenades were the main weapons.

With the air offensive playing a steadily growing part in smashing German communications, the Luftwaffe is putting up a stronger fight than at any time since the landing took place.

Even so, 750 heavy bombers went into action yesterday, and Allied aircraft flew more sorties during the morning than during the whole of Sunday, when an estimated 3,600 planes spearheaded by 1,000 American heavy bombers, dropped thousands of tons of explosives on targets in France.

These formations smashed at German guns, troops, convoys, communications and airfields from the beach-heads to Paris, and as far north as the Pas de Calais area. Observers trying to assess the pattern of our attack on communications say we are slowly splitting the northern coast of France into two halves separated by a wedge of destruction driven right up the Seine to the Paris region.

In addition, Berlin was bombed Sunday night for the third night running by a force of Mosquitos. Synchronised with Sunday's other attacks were assaults launched at German coastal guns in the Pas de Calais area, first major onslaught on this much-bombed region since the start of the landings.

Air umbrella

At the same time, fighters flew a protective umbrella over the beach-heads, and naval forces lying off the coasts, while other fighters and fighter-bombers struck at tactical targets ranging from solitary dispatch riders to tank concentrations.

Throughout the day Spitfires landed and took off from landing strips newly-built behind the Allied lines in France. These, it was learnt at S.H.A.E.F. yesterday, are also being used by Thunderbolts.

British and American warships have again been used against enemy positions in the northern part of the Cherbourg peninsula, Sidney Mason, Reuter's special correspondent at Supreme Headquarters.

TURN TO PAGE 4

'..To the end.'

GENERAL MONTGOMERY has sent the following personal message to troops of the 21st Army Group: "After four days of fighting Allied armies have secured a good and firm lodgement area on the mainland of France.

"First, we must thank Almighty God for the success we have achieved and for giving us such a good beginning towards the full completion of our task. Second, we must pay tribute to the Allied navies and air forces for their magnificent co-operation and support. Without it we soldiers could have achieved nothing.

"Third, I want personally to congratulate every officer and man in the Allied Army on the splendid results of the last four days. British, Canadian and American soldiers fighting gallantly side by side have achieved great success and have placed themselves in a good position from which to exploit this success.

"To every officer and man whatever may be his rank or employment, I send my grateful thanks and my best wishes for the future.

"Much still remains to be done; but together, you and I, we will do it, and we will see the thing through to the end. Good luck to you all." Signed, B. L. Montgomery, Commander-in-Chief, 21st Army Group, France.

In a special message to the Commander, 50 (Northumbrian) Division, General Montgomery expressed his "heartfelt congratulations on the achievement of 50 Division, to yourself and all ranks."

The Corps Commander adds his congratulations. His message said: "All our objectives have been gained and vigorous reconnaissance thrusts are now proceeding towards vital spots. Well done indeed. Grand lads!! champion!!!"

Springboks in surprise move

THE action of Sixth South African Armoured Division in the Liri and Sacco Valleys, where it distinguished itself in heavy fighting round Genazzano, and its rapid surprise move through Rome to the north-west were revealed officially yesterday. It was also stated officially that the German Fourteenth Army is scattered.

The enemy has been cleared from the whole area south of the Pescara River and Avezzano and neighbouring villages occupied by New Zealanders.

In the central sector, our troops are advancing towards Rieti, said yesterday's communique, while west of the Tiber the important road junction of Montefiascone, south-east of Lake Bolsena, is in our hands.

On the coast leading elements are approaching Orbetello, which is due west of Viterbo.

Troops of an Indian division are across the Pescara, after having occupied the town of the same name, while farther south the villages of Villamagna and Pacentro have been taken.

Referring to the Sixth South African Division, it was officially stated yesterday that on the fall of Rome it was decided to pass the Division through formations of the Fifth Army and to initiate a drive north-west of the Tiber.

The Division moved rapidly and in close co-operation with formations of the Fifth Army, through which it passed under most difficult conditions, crossed the Tiber and pushed rapidly north-west.

"This," it was stated, "is another instance of a ghost move by Eighth Army which has so frequently in the past surprised and perplexed the enemy."

The Division drove the enemy back and took the town of Civita Castellana. Then, on June 10, they had a most successful battle north of Viterbo. A number of enemy tanks and self-propelled guns were destroyed and more than 200 Germans killed. The Division is now more than 50 miles from Rome.

"It is now quite clear that the original Fourteenth Army of General Von Mackensen has been dispersed to the four winds," said an official spokesman. "All

that remains is a few scattered remnants which are mainly engaged in stealing one another's transport in order to get away as fast as possible. Prisoners describe the situation as wholly chaotic."

Most striking evidence of the degree of disintegration is provided by the fact that stragglers from the army have been captured who are provided with official passes stating "Bearer of this pass is

TURN TO PAGE 4

Soviet drive on Finland

RUSSIAN penetration of the defences of the Karelian isthmus—the battle-ground of the Russo-Finnish war of 1939-40—has already reached a depth, in places, of 15 miles on a front of 25 miles.

The Red Army is well on the way to Viborg, focal point of the heaviest fighting of the earlier war, which is astride the road to Helsinki, Finland's capital.

The blow has been delivered on this front just two months after the break-down of the Soviet-Finnish peace talks.

Stalin's Order of the Day announcing the opening of the offensive ends with a variant of the usual Soviet reference by saying: "Death to the German-Finnish invaders."

General Govorov's crack guards, supported by massed artillery and wave after wave of first-line aircraft, are grinding down enemy opposition.

Eighty inhabited places were occupied in the early stages of the attack. These included the key point of Terijoki, 15 miles west of the Russo-Finnish frontier of 1939.

A Reuter message from Moscow says: "Once it was clear the Finns were unwilling to accept the Soviet terms the master plan came out

bombardments from land and air have been abandoned. Many prisoners were taken and much booty captured. Ships of the Baltic Fleet are supporting our offensive.—Reuter.

Pacific isles battered

A POWERFUL Pacific fleet on Saturday attacked enemy positions on Saipan, Tinian and Guam islands in the Marianas with carrier aircraft, according to an announcement issued by the U.S. Navy Department.

General MacArthur's communique, issued in New Guinea yesterday, announced that Liberators of the 5th Air Force destroyed 22 Japanese planes over Palau in the Carolines and sank eight Japanese ships at Manokwari, west of Biak Island.

The U.S. air forces also struck again at Truk, dropping 60 tons of bombs on the Japanese airport and seaplane bases there. Three intercepting Japanese fighters were shot down for the loss of one Allied plane.

The British *Union Jack* during the Normandy landings.

Which is secretly rather a bore.
Our women, God bless 'em, their pluck never fails,
Serving out Horlicks to combatant males,
Though the rust on the teaspoons has ruined their nails,
They're doing their bit for the war.

Fighting for freedom in Simla,
Democracy's cause we defend;
With people to tea
From W.S.C.,

103

Cover of *Laugh with Seac*.

What curious people they send!!
Fighting for freedom in Simla,
Doing our share and much more
We'd like to be back in our country so dear.
One day we'll return there – of that never fear
When the Germans are not so exceedingly near!
We'll be doing our bit for the War.

D.W.A.

NEWSREEL

The river softly ran between
The jungle, Japless, calm, serene –

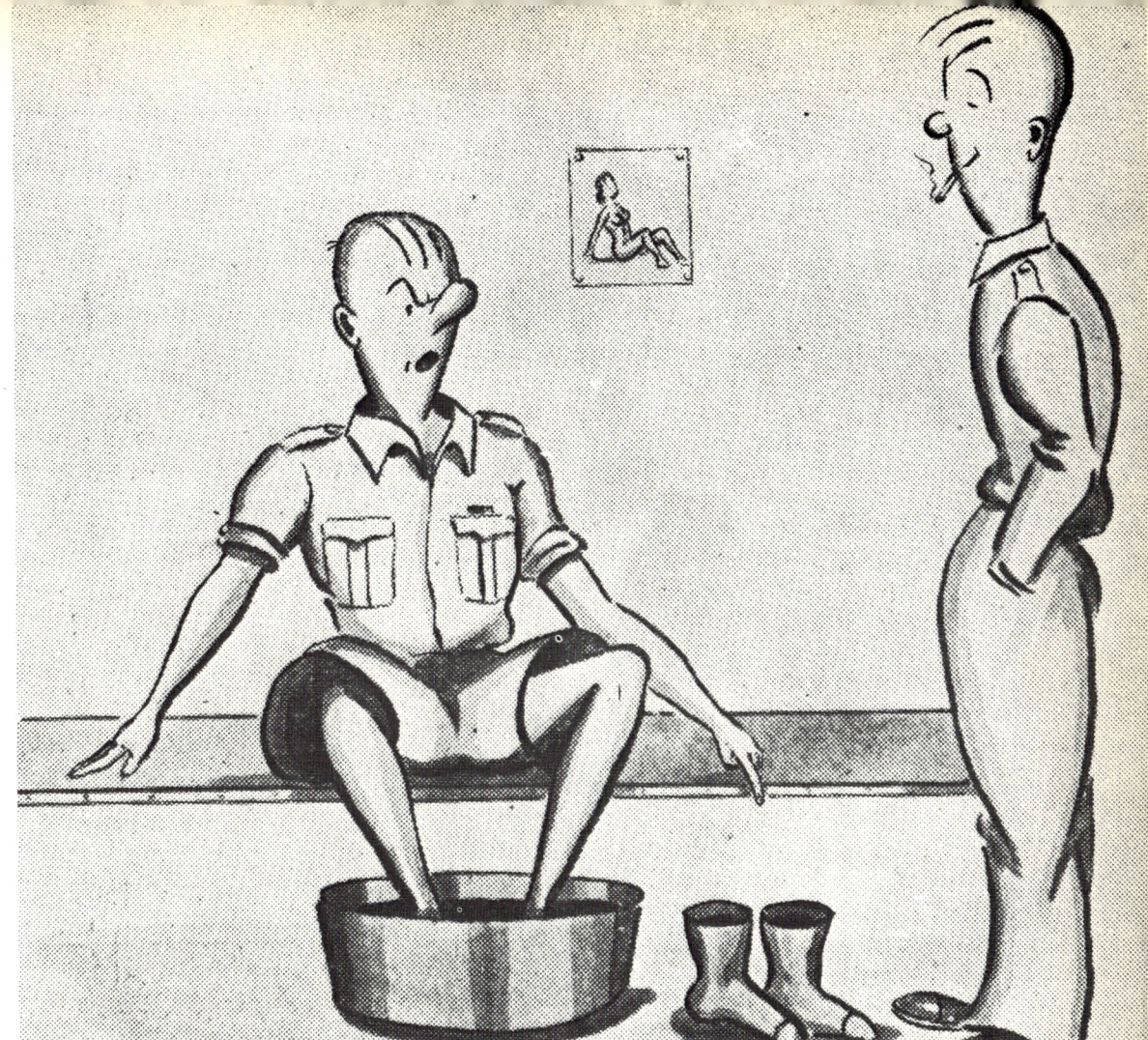

'Mosquito boots nothin'! Them's M E S O C K S!' The privations of service life by Anglo from *Seac*.

The Colonel ordered: 'Fun, good, clean;
Send for film unit, mobile.'
We sent. They came and cleared a space
of trees, except a useful brace
To hold a sheet to frame the face
of Garbo, full or profile.
A Donald Duck delighted first
With sound track rather unrehearsed,
The operator roundly cursed –
He showed it upside down.
Then last year's Movietone, the best
Showed Indians at the Sahibs' behest
Landing in Italy – the icy West
The announcer went to town.
He said, 'It's cold: look, I declare
They're issued with warm clothes to wear
The first thing that they do is . . .' There
The sound track leapt its socket:
The words were, had he got them out,
'Is put it on,' without a doubt –
But his were drowned by Cockney shout:
'The first they do is "flog" it.'

Ikki

105

'That's the blood of them there beetles they chew.' *Seac*.

GONGED

For growing a belly,
Campaigning in Delhi,
   I earned the Medal (Defence);
And the Italy Star
Was for running a bar
   Away from the front in Florence.
Thirty-nine forty-five
I got in a 'dive'
   Unpleasantly close to Calcutta;
Whilst the Africa Star

106

(The hardest by far)
  Was for dishing out tea, bread and butter.
To complete my full row,
I took part in a show
  (Armed with my knife, fork and spoon)
When running a camp
In the heat and the damp
  And the terrors and trials of Rangoon.

Ffortescue

LIEUTENANT'S LAMENT

I've petted hard with Pam way back in Poona,
I've messed around with Margie in Madras,
And on furlough in Mussoorie
Was a burning, yearning houri
Over whom I made myself an awful ass.
I've kissed Kate in a kishtie up in Kashmir,
Made lurid love to Lucy in Lahore,
While in dear Old Rawalpindi
There was pretty, witty Lindy
Who took all that I could give – then asked for more.
I've made amatory aims at Anne in Agra,
Sat side by side with Sheila in Shillong,
And last year in Maynamatti
I met stunning, cunning Patty
Who knew all there was to know of right – and wrong.
I'm bound to find a bint or two in Burma,
(Maybe upon the Road to Mandalay);
But I fear I am contrary
For I long for my sweet Mary
Who is just about eight thousand miles away.

Buttercup

S.E.A.C. LOVE SONG

Oh beautiful Marcia,
Please come to my barcia,
My cosy abode of bambou.
We will get in with ease
Since all the sub-chease
Consists just of me and of you.

Oh please, Marcia, cum
To my hovel ek-dum,
Let me gaze on your loveliness now.
I will cheer to the ekko

107

'I've got to go on manoeuvres
immediately after the dance,
Sally!' *Seac*.

BapS.

For just one small dekko –
So please, sweetest love, idhar ow.

And then when we marry,
In your khaki-drill sarry
The men just to see you will throng.
Oh my own heart's ranee,
Please come jaldi to me –
My hut has been empty too long.

With your figure and garb
You will make a mem-sarb
That would credit a great maharaja.
(We could add grass porticos
To house all our chicos,
As the family grows laja and laja).

Guru

108

SONG OF THE REPATRIATES

(With apologies to Henry Newbolt)

The tea is in Darjeeling an' a thousand miles away,
    (Cha-wallah art thou sleeping there below?)
Keep stiring up the ashes and brewing up all day
    When soldier-lads are bound for Plymouth Hoe.
Yonder lies old England, here lie the ships
    With soldier-lads a-training heel-and-toe,
An' the bearer's feet are flashing and the babu's teeth are
        gnashing
While seasoned troopers drink their cha as they did long ago.

The tea comes from Darjeeling and travels seven seas,
    (Cha-wallah art thou sleeping there below?)
An' when a man is thirsty he drinks eight pints with ease
    Despite the cooling thoughts of Plymouth Hoe.
So take my mug to England, hang it by the door,
    Strike when your cha is running low;
If the bearer sahibs reach Devon,
    I'll quit the port o' Heaven
And have do-anna-cha and wads
    As I did long ago.

'Can't understand you flying
blokes. Like to stay on the
deck myself!' Cartoon by
Power from *Seac*.

SCENES THAT ARE BRIGHTEST

Hindustan, my Hindustan,
    Softly I breathe 'Farewell',
With a gleam in my eye, malicious and vicious,
    Regretful? Or fretful? Like hell!
And now I reflect on the boat deck
    Caressing my Burma cheroot,
And feel just a tearful of sorrow
At leaving my India. My foot!

Scene 1

In the Willingdon Club garden
    On the trees the khidmitgars,
While I eat my fried chaprasis
    In the scent of chowkidars.

Scene 2

Leaving early on shikara
    All agog to chance one's luck
'Neath the bunya trees of Poona
    Wildly shooting Bombay duck.

Scene 3

Sitting on a cushioned bekti
    At Firpo's restaurant in town
With a bottle of masalchi
    Washing jellied kishtis down.

Scene 4

Drinking cool subah saweres
    By the palms of Kalimpong,
Buying pots from paniwalas
    In bazaars at Chittagong.

Epilogue

Hindustan, my Hindustan,
    'Farewell' must end my letter,
Pray God that very soon I shall fare better.

Jackdaw

On and Off Parade

A review of features, articles, and stories which appeared in service publications of World War II illustrates the wide range of material – humorous and serious – offered to soldiers, sailors, and airmen wherever they served. Features made them familiar with the work of all branches of the services and their service conditions, kept them politically aware, and helped them formulate and develop ideas for the future. Some of the features were written by war correspondents of national newspapers, some by reporters of service publications, and some by ordinary servicemen in their 'free' time. Others were by politicians, civilians, and 'experts'. Short stories, many of them by well-known authors, were reprinted or were specially written for publication in service newspapers and magazines, and, of course, servicemen made their various contributions on a free-lance basis.

Today, perhaps, 'wizard prang', 'bang on', and 'get some in' are unfamiliar terms or sound dated; but there are millions who must still remember that once they were 'browned off' or 'chokker', that things were 'too true' or 'up the creek' and that they never said 'Let's have a look' but 'Let's have a shufti' or 'Let's have a dekko', in the days when sausages were 'snorkers', 'bangers', or 'soya links'. They must remember, too, that they never let a day go by without saying, at least a dozen times, 'Roll on duration' or 'Roll on demob.' And always they were asking 'What's the latest gen?' or 'What's the latest griff?' Service publications supplied many of the answers.

The war still had a long way to go when, early in 1940, an officer cadet wrote an article in *Battle Dress* entitled 'London Weekends – notes on where to eat drink and make merry in war-time London'. The information was not much use to the rank and file, whose army pay was fourteen shillings per week, less two shillings compulsorily deducted for 'barrack room damages' and seven shillings allotment to wife or parents. Even in those days the licentious soldiery could not go raving mad on five shillings per week take-back-to-billets pay.

The cadet complained that lots of people were finding a 'Saturday-Sunday in Town' expensive, and that even the Lyons Corner House and Regent Palace routine was not cheap and was monotonous anyway. He breezily stated that he had 'dropped in Chez Filliez', twenty yards up Frith Street from Shaftesbury Avenue, where the food was cosmopolitan and the cooking French. A first-class meal there cost three and sixpence, smoked salmon cost a shilling and a 'dream of an entrecote' topped with a lump of butter sauce was one shilling and fourpence. The young cadet also recommended the grilled trout and mushrooms, but did not state the price. For the cadet and millions of others harder times were just ahead.

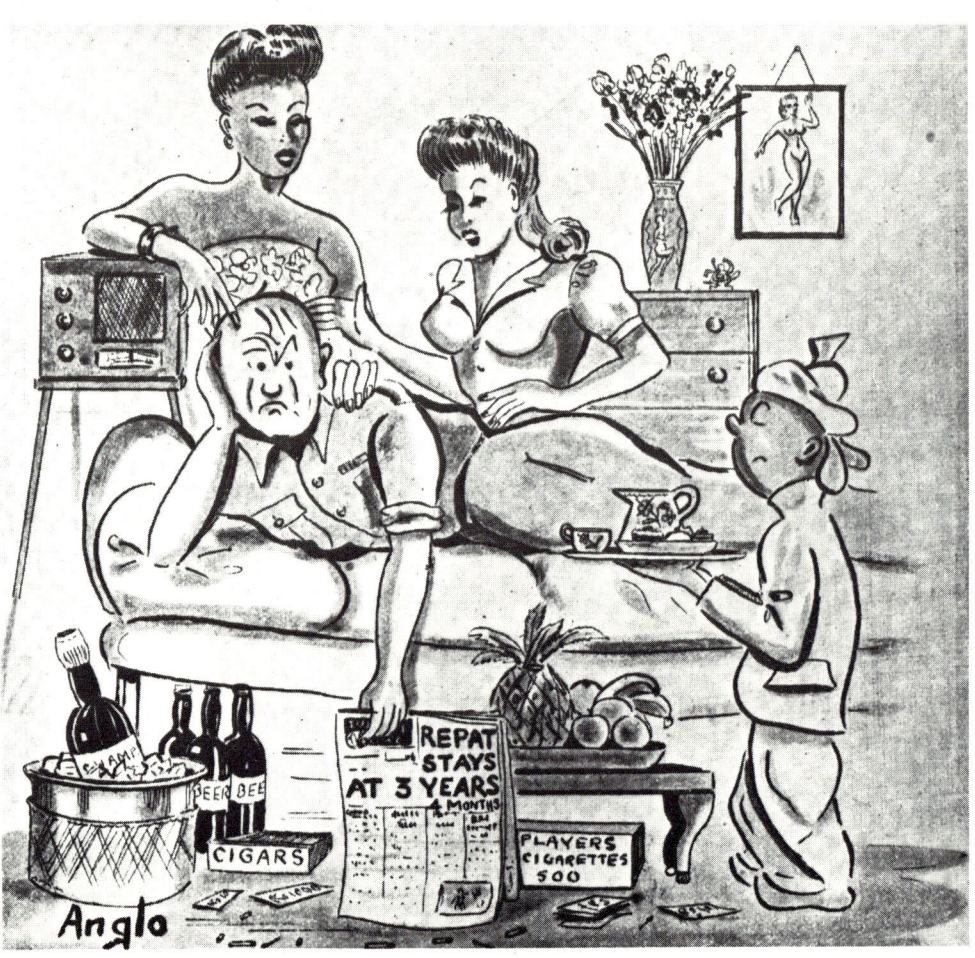

'Welfare 1950' from *Seac*.

With so many men and women in the services, civilian magazines such as *Lilliput*, *Men Only*, and *Picture Post* were angled to encompass service readership. Most servicemen saw these publications in Naafis, service reading rooms and canteens at home, but not often abroad. The cartoons, short stories, and picture features based on service life were popular and their style was followed in service magazines such as *Parade* in the Middle East, *Victory* in India, and, much later, by *Soldier* in Europe. Service newspapers printed on the presses of foreign newspapers, and usually following their format, came in all shapes and sizes as the papers moved with the armies. Despite shortages of materials, air raids, and numerous other difficulties, the service publications always managed to maintain a good standard with

'Honest, mate, I couldn't resist it – it's the first ruddy chain I've pulled for four years.' *Seac*.

interesting content and, for the most part, a reasonable physical product.

Most of the large-circulation service newspapers did not appear until a few years after the war had started, but they were big morale-boosters at crucial times. When *Ceylon Review* first made its appearance in September 1942, the Axis had just about reached the zenith of its power. The Germans were hammering at the gates of Stalingrad; they were deep into the Caucasus, and in Egypt were threatening Alexandria; the tide of the Japanese advance was only just beginning to recede, with the Australians on the move in New Guinea and the Americans on Guadalcanal.

Then, from October 1942, the Allied service newspapers had plenty of good news to report. First came the German defeat at El Alamein in that month, followed by the Russian offensive at Stalingrad in November. After that came the Allied landings in North Africa. In Burma, where there was no Fourteenth Army in 1942, British and Indian troops were holding the Japanese. In May 1943 came the news that the Chindits of the first Wingate expedition had been operating behind the Japanese lines for three months, and that same month the Germans were kicked out of Tunisia. By October 1943, Italy had surrendered to the Allies, but unrelenting fighting against

PARADE

Vol. 1 — No. 2 — Cairo, August 24, 1940.

In this issue:

GOODBYE, CAPUZZO!
British Navy shells Libya.

IN THE WESTERN DESERT
Map of Libya-Egypt frontier.

15
mi.
(in Eg

On *Parade* – pipes in the Western Desert.

the Germans continued there. In 1944 came the Allied invasion of Normandy, and the liberation of Paris then of France. The battle at Arnhem in Holland and the Battle of the Bulge in the Ardennes were setbacks. In India, after the battles at Kohima and Imphal, the Japanese were on the run. In May 1945 the war in Europe was over, and the Japanese were hammered by the Allies until in August 1945 they too gave up.

Many details of the series of events and fighting over this long period were not reported until a long time after they had actually taken place, and articles about units and formations, policies, and details of movements were often held back for security reasons. Sometimes an item from one service paper or a non-service publication would be reprinted in another service publication at a much later date. But by and large the service papers, despite censorship, kept the troops reasonably well informed.

A story that appeared in service newspapers in South-East Asia in October 1944, without a by-line, recounted the exploits of the Royal Fusiliers at Anzio in January 1943, when the Londoners had fought the Germans bitterly and almost continuously for days on end 'in mud up to their ankles, soaked to the skin, knowing that to fail might mean the complete destruction of the Anzio bridgehead'. That it was the 8th Battalion, Royal Fusiliers, of the famous 56th Black Cat Division that took part in the Anzio landing was not then specified in the article.

In an article praising the British infantry Arthur Bryant declared that the war had restored the British infantryman to the pinnacle he had won at Agincourt, Salamanca, and Waterloo, and that he was no longer 'the fool who walked behind the artillery to be killed'. A cynical infantrymen reading this flattering article probably agreed. Now he was the stooge who walked behind the tanks to be killed. Of one thing he was certain: he never had to walk behind the generals to be killed. He must have marvelled when he read about his superlative physical fitness, instinctive battle discipline, natural and flexible, and his assured mastery of weapons and vehicles, his quickness in movement, his quick thinking, and his spirit of individual awareness and initiative 'that should be proof against all mishaps on the swiftly changing battlefield today'. Proof against bombs, shells, and bullets? Much of what Bryant said was true, although the infantryman would never admit it, and since flattery boosted morale it was dished out in dollops.

Men in every branch of the services were always interested in the work of specialist units such as Commandos, the Special Air Service, the Commando Special Boat Service, Frogmen, Chindits, and Para-troops. Service publications ran many articles and photo features about their work and exploits, especially in the latter years of the war.

Numerous articles about Commandos appeared in service publications over the war years. One of these, 'Commandos Began

'Articles and photo features.'
A North African soldier
pictured in the Kaladar
Valley, Burma.

in Mayfair' by Lieut. E. G. Grove ('the inside story of the Army's "Irregulars"'), appeared in *Soldier* on 4 August 1945, more than five years after their inception. Grove dispelled many myths about the Special Service troops and told about the first Commando raid, which had taken place on 23 June 1940, on the coast of France between Cap d'Alprech near Boulogne and the Pointe du Hautbanc near Berck, when R.A.F. 'crash-boats' were used to carry the raiders to and from France.

The saga of the S.A.S. started in 1941 in the Desert, when the idea of hand-picked specialists operating behind enemy lines was evolved by two young British officers, Lieut. David Sterling, Scots Guards and Commandos, and Lieut. Jock Lewis, Welsh Guards and Commandos. The story of the S.A.S. was told briefly several years after its formation, and even then readers were reminded that the exploits of the romantic unit whose motto was 'Who Dares, Wins' could never be fully recounted until after the war, if then.

John Hallows, a staff writer on *Soldier* magazine, wrote an article about the work of British frogmen 'who made our D-Day landings possible'. The article was reprinted in several service publications including *Ceylon Review* and *Seac*, which devoted a centre spread to a condensed version of the article together with several photographs. The training and employment of frogmen had been a closely kept secret. They had tackled the undersea defences of the Western Wall and cleared the way to the Normandy beaches for the invaders. Frogmen were already at the Commando Camp near Jaffna, Ceylon, training for the assault on Malaya and Singapore when the article appeared and were well known to Army and Marine Commandos, who greeted the 'bullshit' story with the usual service ribaldry.

Service newspapers published many stories about the Chindits from the beginning of 1943 when news of their exploits first appeared in the press all over the world. 'Chindit' was an anglicized form of *Chinthé*, the Burmese word for a griffin-like lion, and was inadvertently coined by Orde Wingate. The term was first used in the *Daily Express*, when Alaric Jacob referred to Maj.-Gen. Orde Wingate's specially trained brigade as the Chindits. This brigade, made up of a battalion of the King's (Liverpool) and a battalion of Gurkha Rifles and Burma Rifles, left Imphal for the first Wingate expedition, and crossed the Chindwin into Japanese-occupied territory. They were entirely dependent on air drops for supplies. Subsequently, Airborne Chindits took part in extended operations behind the enemy lines, where they played havoc, wrecking railways and depots and cutting Japanese communications. A first-hand account of the Chindits by Maj. M. T. Booth was one of a number that appeared in service publications. Another account was included in an unsigned article headlined 'The Men of the Fourteenth' which was about units of the Fourteenth Army, many of which had trained in the jungles of Ceylon before moving up to Burma. The units mentioned which had trained in Ceylon included the East African Divisional Scouts who acted as jungle Commandos in the Kaladan Valley, S.O.G.s such as the Commando S.B.S., and Coppists, Marine Commandos, and U.S. specialist units.

The Fourteenth Army had come to be known as the 'Forgotten Army' while efforts were concentrated on supplying the forces fighting in Europe. Non-service newspapers at home rarely mentioned the forces in South-East Asia until the war in Europe was nearly over, and even then they never seemed to get it quite right. On 21 August 1945 the editorial column of *Seac* quoted a letter from a senior officer in the Fourteenth Army just returned from sixty-one days leave in the United Kingdom:

In the UK I travelled throughout the country by road and rail, and I stayed for periods in London and other large cities. I found everywhere a dreadful ignorance about the Fourteenth Army, and also generally about Burma. The Fourteenth Army flash means nothing to the average Briton. Many times I was asked was I an Australian or a New Zealander because of my bush-hat.

Following General Slim's wonderful reception in the

117

Guildhall all the dailies featured 'Bill Slim and his gallant Fourteenth'; but the *Times*, in an otherwise blameless editorial referred to the 'Belgian infantry' that had shared the victories in Burma; the *Daily Dispatch* referred to a 'batch of Australian soldiers wearing the Fourteenth Army flash' present in the body of the Guildhall.

It was part of the job of service newspapers in South-East Asia to publicize the work and deeds of S.E.A.C., and this they did stoutly with such articles as 'Tribute to the Fighting Fourteenth' by Victor Thompson. They also did much to publicize Lieut.-Gen. William Slim, the man who had built the Fourteenth Army.

In an article entitled 'Fantastic Odds Beaten by British 14th Army', written from London and appearing in *Maple Leaf* on Wednesday, 27 December 1944, Robert Petty stated:

> If you think the Italian front is tough read this story of the Burma Campaign: 'Problems of Supply and Health Staggering'. I have learned some of the facts from the services newspaper *Seac Souvenir* which says 'a half million men lived and fought in the jungle: how they even lived there is one of the miracles of the war.'

On Tuesday, 9 October 1945, *Seac* quoted from a leader printed in the *Daily Telegraph* which praised the achievements of the Fourteenth Army. 'Armies, like captains and Kings, depart when wars are over,' the article said. 'The Eighth Army has for some time ceased to exist. The Fourteenth, equally famous, is now to be abolished and replaced by a Malaya Command.' *Seac* announced at the same time that the British Fourteenth Army, soon to be known as the Malaya Command, were to be given Sunday off.

The Supremo of South-East Asia Command had always done everything possible to see that his men were not forgotten. A Crown Film Unit was sent to Ceylon at the end of 1944 to make a film, to be shown in Britain, of Royal Marines doing jungle training. One of the cameramen, Denny Densham, wrote a short article about the assignment for service papers, which was reprinted in the national press. He said that the film had turned out to be one of the toughest assignments that he had been given and that even his share of making *Western Approaches* was put in the shade. In making a Royal Marine Commando film, *By Sea and Land*, he had imagined he had come up against nature in the raw when he spent ten days in a front-line dugout in France, but compared to the location in Ceylon all others had been absolute heaven. Yet he admitted that he had experienced only a little discomfort compared to what troops in Burma had to face, and there had been no real fighting to do.

The versatility of the Royal Marine was a byword. Marines had served on A.A. batteries ashore, in gun-turrets of warships, and had manned assault craft of every description in every theatre of war where

LORD MOUNTBATTEN VISITS BEACH COMMANDOS OF R.I.N. Admiral Lord Louis Mountbatten, Supreme Allied Commander, South East Asia, inspected a Beach Commando unit of the R.I.N. Here he is seen talking to an R.I.N. Beach Commando rating.

The Supreme Commander stopped frequently to talk to individual officers and men.

The C-in-C in India, General Sir Claude Auchinleck, inspecting the men of a mine-sweeper during his Calcutta area tour.

combined operations had taken place. Royal Marine Commandos landed in Normandy on D-Day. They held the Orne bridgehead with the Sixth Airborne Division and had pushed eastwards against the Seine to the Havre–Dieppe coast. It was Royal Marine Commandos who had played an important part in the capture of the island of Walcheren on the Scheldt, landing at West Kapelle, one of the most difficult landings of the war, extinguishing the German batteries and linking up with the 52nd Lowland Division along the south-western rim of the island.

In January 1945, Royal Marines of the East Indies Fleet assaulted the Jap-occupied island of Cheduba off the Burmese coast, the first time that ship-borne Marines had been the landing force in a combined operation, which was in fact an all-naval operation.

Royal Marine Commandos were given their share of deserved

119

publicity in an article by *Daily Telegraph* correspondent Richard Legge about an unusual campaign against the Germans fought by British soldiers, sailors, and airmen and by Marshal Tito's partisans in the Adriatic and along the Dalmatian coast throughout the latter part of 1943 and the spring and summer of 1944. Legge said that there were two important reasons why the fullest publicity should now be given to the campaign. The first was that it had played an important part in the Allies' Mediterranean strategy, and had been made up of a series of vivid episodes in which British servicemen had displayed skill and daring which deserved to be perpetuated. The second reason was that British reticence and the need for security had hitherto kept in wraps the magnitude of what had been done to assist a partner in the fight against the enemy.

Legge told the story of the big raid when nearly six thousand British and Partisan infantry were landed on the island of Brac as a diversion intended to draw off some of the German forces driving against Tito's headquarters in Yugoslavia. After this successful operation the raiders withdrew to Vis. Among the troops who took part were No. 2 Commando, two Royal Marine Commandos, a battalion of Highlanders, gunners of a field regiment, a raiding support regiment, and some American O.G. troops as well as a formation of partisans.

Legge's article, which was reprinted in service publications, was the first intimation thousands of servicemen had of such operations, though it appeared long after the Germans had evacuated Dalmatia. It concluded with the words inscribed on a tablet raised by Brigadier Churchill in the little cemetery by Vis harbour:

> After more than 100 years British sailors and soldiers who fought and died for their Country's honour on the seas and islands of Dalmatia have again been laid to rest in this island cemetery – 1944.

Daily Express correspondent Alan Wood, who was at Arnhem throughout the battle to secure a bridgehead across the Neder Rhine in September 1944, gave his stark account of the Airborne landings and the subsequent disastrous events culminating in the British withdrawal:

> This is the history of the First British Airborne Division at Arnhem. I give it here as I wrote it from day to day. It is not the complete story. This will never be known. It was a battle of unknown heroes, with our division becoming split up into isolated groups, cut off without contact with headquarters, fighting on with no hope of supplies or reinforcements, until each man was killed or wounded or captured. I can only tell the story of the particular group I was with; and we had the easiest time of any. We were the lucky ones. We got away.

Union Jack, Christmas issue, 1944.

UNION JACK

Issued free to the British Fighting Forces.

SPECIAL TWELVE-PAGE
CHRISTMAS ISSUE, 1944

Monday, December 25, 1944.

TO-DAY

We drink a toast to our Allies

INSIDE: *The story of Bethlehem . . . other Army Christmases recalled . . . a year of triumph on the battlefields . . . What 1944 has meant to our fighting men . . . Christmas Eve at the local . . . Special Quiz . . . Damon Runyon . . . Messages to the folks at Home . . . Our own ghost story . . . Peter Wilson's sporting memories . . . George Maracco . . . AND, interrupting everywhere, the TWO TYPES spend Christmas with you.*

Alan Wood's simple and graphic story, reprinted in service publications, was read by British and American servicemen in every theatre of war. Of his part in the actual evacuation from the perimeter at Oosterbeek, he wrote:

> The withdrawal, called operation 'Berlin' is to be made by small groups. Our major, Roy Oliver, has the job of getting our little Public Relations bunch, a mixed bag consisting of three unarmed war correspondents, two censors armed with blue pencils, three cameramen, four radio operators, and an R.A.F. radar expert . . .
>
> No need to bother about destroying equipment; nearly everything we had was smashed long ago in the shelling. But I have broken up my typewriter with a pickaxe so that no *Voelkischer Beobachter* war correspondent ever uses it.

A later article, which appeared in several service magazines, told the story of the unsung heroes of the Arnhem battle, the 250 men of the Dorset Regiment who had smashed through the German lines and made the hazardous crossing of the Lek River to reach the beleaguered men of the First Airborne Division with supplies, and then had held on until the evacuation of the 2,800 Airborne survivors was completed. Few of the Dorsets got back.

Another story of the British Airborne in action was told by Joe Illingsworth about the men of the famous Sixth Airborne Division fighting in the Ardennes at the tip of Runstedt's 'bulge' in December 1944, and their bloody battle in the German-held village of Bure in bitter wintry conditions. The British paratroopers, using sten-guns, Tommy guns, and Piats and, at close quarters, knives, had fought against German self-propelled guns, artillery, mortars, and Tiger tanks. As at Arnhem, the battle had raged from house to house and from garden to garden.

Servicemen thousands of miles away in warmer climes read about Bure and the Ardennes and wondered whether they would like to be fighting like their comrades closer to home. If there had been a choice, it was Hobson's.

For generations young Gurkhas had left their homes in Nepal for their traditional adventure of serving in the Indian Army with the British forces along the North West Frontier from the snowy peaks of Chitral to the Khyber and the Bolan and along the North East Frontier and in Burma. The Gurkhas were always popular with British soldiers who knew them in the Western Desert, Italy, the Arakan, and Burma. Never British subjects, these hardy little hillmen are among the toughest soldiers in the world, and they fought by the side of the British in some of the fiercest engagements of both world wars. Their reputation as redoubtable fighters and their deadly precision with their national weapon, the kukri, a heavy, eighteen-inch curved steel blade, scared the wits out of Germans, Italians, and Japanese.

'Redoubtable fighters';
Gurkhas served in many
theatres of war. *Fauji Akhbar*,
19 December 1944.

ABOVE (left): A Gurkha patrol is briefed by the N.C.O. and (right) a scout in front of a Gurkha patrol gives the signal for the main body to advance.

Gurkha Patrol on Adriatic Sector of Italian Front

The weather continues to bog down the 8th Army in the Adriatic sector, but minor advances continue. These pictures were taken by a photographer who accompanied a Gurkha patrol on a sortie against an enemy outpost.

Service newspapers in particular were pleased to carry stories of the exploits of Gurkhas in Europe, the Middle East, and South-East Asia. They won numerous military awards, including many V.C.s, and tales (true and apocryphal) of their phenomenal bravery were legion. Among the many articles about these fabulous fighters was one by a Gurkha, Paresh Nath, entitled 'The Little Men with the Big Knives' and first published in *Star Weekly Toronto* in 1944. Another, by *Daily Sketch* military correspondent Brig. E. C. Anstey, D.S.O., was reprinted in several service newspapers. *Fauji Akhbar* was read by Gurkhas and published many items of special interest for them. Two oft-repeated apocryphal tales sum up their reputation: Airborne Gurkha troops dropped into battle, only to learn later they were

123

German army magazine – *Die Wehrmacht*.

supposed to use parachutes. An enemy soldier encountered a kukri-wielding Gurkha, who took a swing at him. 'Missed!' shouted the enemy. 'Try shaking your head,' replied the grinning Gurkha.

As a public relations exercise service newspapers often featured profiles on various native types encountered by servicemen, sometimes resorting to semi-humorous features couched in affectionate terms in an effort to foster goodwill among the rude soldiery. Such was an article written by Gerald E. Schluter for servicemen in East Africa from Nairobi, Harrar, and Hersein to Mogadishu.

From the outset of 1941, the forces of General Cunningham had attacked the Italian East African empire from the three directions of Eritrea, Somaliland, and the Sudanese-Abyssinian border. By March 1941 Eritrea had fallen, the final victory being the successful assault by the Indian Army on the mountain fortress of Keren. On 6 April, the Abyssinian capital, Addis Ababa, was captured and the surrender of Gondar on 27 November marked the elimination of Italy's empire in East Africa. The aftermath of battle left the British forces in close contact with a large number of Abyssinian, Somali, and Eritrean tribes.

Schluter's article dealt with Hussein Bin Mohamed, dubbed 'Hussein the talented, the "wily Somale"', who had brought a multitude of talents to the war in East Africa. According to Schluter, Hussein was a good guide, an admirable interpreter 'who spoke a little English and an untold number of native languages; was a good judge of character who could adapt the usual Somali flair for intrigue for the needs of his job and had a good nose for a profitable deal, too.' British troops had no need to be reminded of the hundreds of Husseins with whom they had to deal. They had their own opinions, most of which were not printable.

By the time the Russians swept into Poland on 17 September 1939, the German army had practically wiped up the Polish forces and would have had less difficulty in pushing on to the Russian frontier than it had a year later. A typical contemporary headline in the British press was 'The Soviet plays Jackal to the Nazi Lion.' And nobody asked what the British lion had been doing for Poland until then, besides dropping leaflets over Germany. Russia was reviled and blamed for the Polish débâcle.

With the Russian invasion of Finland, on 3 November 1939, to forestall the Germans doing a deal with Mannerheim, the press took the side of 'gallant little Finland', becoming especially vociferous as appalling weather slowed down the Russian advance and, for a while, it seemed more than likely that British troops would be sent through neutral Norway or even Sweden to aid the Finns. Anti-Russian sentiment, stirred up with the invasion of Poland, was whipped up as Russian bombers raided Finland and newspapers and magazines in Britain told stories of Russian atrocities, incompetence, poor equipment, low morale, and how right we had been not to enlist their aid to counter Germany before the outbreak of war. Little

125

attention was given to the fact that Russia might yet one day be our ally and Finland our enemy. The papers gloated that 'the Red conscripts were blinded by the snow and terrified by the perpetual gloom of the winter forests'. In January 1940, a photograph of Russian prisoners of war was captioned 'Dejected, ill clad and worse shod they were far from being the sort of men who go to make an invincible army.' Soldiers reading this sort of propaganda, especially those on stand-by to be sent to Finland, wondered about the Russians. Those who had hoped and were still hoping that Russia would be our ally were bitterly disappointed.

This attitude changed, of course, when Germany inevitably invaded Russia, but as the Germans burst through Russian-occupied Poland into Russia, sweeping whole Russian armies before them and inflicting colossal losses in men and material, nobody was surprised, in view of the past press reports on the Russian difficulties in the Finnish campaign, and the consensus of opinion in the forces was that 'the Germans would go through the Russians like a dose of salts', an opinion which was even encouraged by the bolder big brass.

When the Russians began to hold the Germans, however, and in some cases take the initiative, the press changed course again, and soon admiration of the Russian soldier was the order of the day. By the time it became clear that in Russia the Germans had the tiger by the tail, British servicemen, pleased that they might not, after all, have to confront the Germans on their own, were already referring to Stalin as 'good old Uncle Joe', as if he had personally come to their aid. But what sort of people were the Russians, really? This was a question often asked by servicemen. It was a question answered from time to time in most service publications, one way or another.

In one service article, 'What Manner of Men are These', Edward Crankshaw pronounced the Russian soldier to be dogged, hard as nails, ruthless in anger, yet cheerful, boundlessly hospitable, and a lover of music and of laughter. Crankshaw sketched the background of the Russians in wartime and the most noticeable characteristics of the Russian people: their capacity for endurance, their unquenchable passion for the dramatic, the colourful, and the musical, their instinct towards sinking the individual for the whole. He added that they were generous, kindly, and determined to preserve a way of life which, with infinite labour and at the cost of unimaginable suffering, they were beginning 'to conquer for themselves when the arch-destroyer struck to snatch it from them'.

The majority of service readers had never heard of Russians such as those described by Crankshaw. What had happened to the Russians of Poland and Finland of a year or two before? They would be resuscitated by the end of the war. But in the meantime, as a sop to the Russophobes and a veiled warning to the Russophiles, there were articles proclaiming that Russia was no longer as far to the left as it had been in the past. In fact, for working-class servicemen who regarded Communist Russia as Utopia and Russians almost as

The battle-scarred heroine comes home in this Navy issue of *Yank*.

BRITISH EDITION

YANK

THE ARMY WEEKLY

3d JAN. 17 1943
VOL. 1, NO. 51

By the men .. for the men in the service

A HEROINE COMES HOME. The battle-scarred cruiser San Francisco enters the harbor of the city for which she was named. Repairs were necessary following her remarkable performance against much heavier Japanese ships off Guadalcanal.

NAVY ISSUE

paragons of virtuous frugality, a short article by Ralph Hewins about Russian millionaires was an unsubtle reminder that this was not quite so. Hewins stated that the reward for outstanding service or talents was the same in Russia as anywhere else – a large income – hinting that in the land of equality some were indeed more equal than others. Contrary to a widespread notion, poverty was not a virtue in a Communist state, and there were many rouble millionaires in Russia. Moreover, a white tie and a bottle of 'Bubbly' were not regarded as symbols of shame in the Kremlin, as innumerable foreign envoys could testify. Hewins concluded, 'What the Kremlin thinks today all Russians think tomorrow.'

From *Union Jack*.

Among those he named as millionaires was the writer Alexei Tolstoy, a distant relative of the great novelist, who had received 3,000,000 roubles from the Soviet government, for his world-famous historical novel *Peter the Great*, which was about normal for such a work in the West; and Mihail Sholokhov, author of *Quiet Flows the Don*, was also paid vast sums for his work. Others named by Hewins were film producers Sergei Eisenstein and V. Pudovkin; the brothers Vassiliev, film directors whose lavish parties on a Hollywood scale did not result in accusations that they were 'class traitors or of any other such outmoded nonsense'; tenors Koslovski, Leoshev, Pechkovski, and baritones Pirogov and Reisen.

Hewins also mentioned many manufacturers with big incomes, and posing the question 'What does a Russian Croesus do with his money?' gave his answer: 'He has a villa outside the city; a town flat near his office, a country "dacha". He has one or more cars with a chauffeur, manservant and domestic staff. He feeds and drinks well and entertains his friends. He travels, and even in war-time snatches brief holidays. His womenfolk have furs and jewels.'

Some cynical servicemen, more concerned that back home privilege had not changed with the war, may have thought that this article was a smelly red herring. Many in civvy street had profited before the war, profited during the war, and would continue to profit after the war.

Another important question servicemen wanted answered was 'Would Russia fight Japan?' To the Allied troops the prospect of an invasion of Japan was daunting. Servicemen who had come through hard campaigns in the Desert, Italy, France, and Germany did not relish the thought of an all-out struggle with the fanatical Japanese. It was realized that Russian intervention in the Far East could well shorten the war and save a lot of Allied lives. The Atom bomb was dropped in August 1944. Months earlier an article by Harrison E. Salisbury in *Collier's* was reprinted in several service publications. Salisbury expressed the opinion that, despite the fact that the ordinary Russian, who depended on *Pravda*, *Zveotia*, or *Red Star* for his knowledge of the world, had only recently been told of details of the second war being fought by the Allies, Russia would join in. This was news Allied soldiers, sailors, and airmen wanted to hear.

An article by Ella Winter that appeared in service papers in September 1945 asked 'Is Russia going Right?' Ella Winter wrote that for the thirties Russia spelt co-education, psychological clinics, equality of the sexes, irreligion, and general promiscuity. Moscow had been the Mecca of intellectuals who thought that the family was a false unit. Winter said that now the churches were open, marriage was sacred, and the Soviet girl was rapidly reacquiring femininity. Thousands of women were getting free abortions which were legally performed at hospitals with the best of care, and sex knowledge and hygiene were taught all over the country. This information was no doubt all very interesting, but servicemen glad the war was over and anxious about demobilization were more concerned about what had been going on at home in their absence and wondered what they were going back to. 'Dear John' letters were frequent enough to remind servicemen of some of the facts of life at home. If churches in Russia were open and the Soviet girls had all become Betty Grables and could get a free abortion, 'bully' for them. What about the girl back home?

Troops involved in evacuations early in the war owed a lot to the Navy, and soldiers involved in combined operations knew full well the part played by Navy men on the beaches as well as aboard landing craft. Troops on their way overseas aboard troopships had also seen some of the work of the Navy. They were familiar with naval units whose destroyers, corvettes, and even aircraft-carriers had protected their convoys. They had watched the practice dropping of depth-charges and anti-aircraft practice en route, and some servicemen

129

had even experienced real naval action when their convoys were attacked by enemy submarines or aircraft. Allied servicemen were never left ignorant of naval matters, and service newspapers regularly covered naval activity from the Arctic to the South Seas with articles and features about the work of the Royal Navy and the U.S. navy. Naval battles, the war against U-boats, the patrol work of destroyers, submarines, and M.T.B.s were all featured and were read about by every branch of the services.

Shark Sense

"We've got a working agreement."

The Navy's Bureau of Aeronautics publishes the SENSE pamphlets, illustrated by Lt. Comdr. Robert Osborn. SHARK SENSE points out that sharks are amazingly overrated, there being only three cases of shark bite in all Navy records. The finny monster's reputation has been built up by the movies, feature writers and by the cartoonist who drew this one for YANK.

Drawing by Sgt. Harry Lampert from *Yank*.

The story of two successful patrols by H.M. submarine *Torbay* in the Mediterranean in 1941 was told in an article without a by-line that appeared in several service publications. Commanded by Lieut.-Com. A. C. C. Miers, R.N., who was subsequently awarded the Victoria Cross for further exploits, the *Torbay*, nineteen days at sea on her first patrol, destroyed two enemy tankers, three caiques, and one schooner, possibly damaged another merchantman, and sank a destroyer. The submarine left Alexandria twelve days later for a second patrol during which she accounted for a submarine, two merchant ships, three schooners, and four caiques carrying German troops. The *Torbay* was one of two submarines which after the fall of Rangoon in 1945 carried a force which included COPP 3 on a twelve-hundred-mile voyage from Trincomalee to reconnoitre Puket Island, a large island held by Thais and Japanese.

The transfer of British naval strength to the Far East gave rise to many problems of a non-operational nature very different from those encountered in the North Sea, the Atlantic, and the

"On reconsidering, corporal, maybe you'd better increase my insurance to $10,000!"

Cartoon by Sgt. Frank Brandt from *Yank*.

Mediterranean. Ian Morrison, *Times* correspondent with the Eastern Fleet, wrote an article highlighting the problems which was subsequently reprinted in *Ceylon Review* on 2 December 1944 and read by many British soldiers, airmen, and American servicemen, as well as by men of the Royal Navy and the Merchant Navy. The article dealt with the methods of coping with the terrific temperatures that developed inside ships in the tropics, especially when they were blacked out at night or closed down for action; problems of health and diet in the tropics; the problems of recreational facilities for the men ashore; general welfare and the lack of privacy at sea. Most sailors were familiar with these problems. Soldiers and airmen with problems of their own to contend with, who usually reserved their sympathy for submariners, were reminded that it was not all

131

'Sorry, Major, but what can you expect in group seventy-five?' *Seac*.

'rum, bum and gramophone' in the Navy, as some Army men serving as A.A. gunners aboard troopers and merchantmen already knew.

Published in *Ceylon Review* on 7 April 1945 was the story of a British submarine serving in Eastern waters which was crippled in a duel with enemy ships and had to run back to base on the surface, beating off repeated attacks by Japanese aircraft. The submarine was commanded by Lieut. D. Swanston, D.S.C. and Bar, of the Royal Navy. His crew suffered sixteen casualties before meeting with a sister ship which towed the battered submarine into harbour. She had been a sitting target for the Japanese for two days, during which time she fought off twenty-five attacks by Japanese seaplanes, bombers, and

'I suppose all that you men think about is war.' *Seac*.

fighter-bombers, shot down a seaplane and damaged at least four other aircraft, survived 'near misses' by bombs, and was raked with fire from cannons and machine-guns. Most of the crew were 'hostilities only' ratings, many of them on their first patrol. Contrary to the popular belief that all submariners were volunteers, many were conscripts.

A naval observer spent a week with the East Indies fleet as it cruised up and down the coast of Sumatra shelling ports and sinking coastal craft. Planes from aircraft-carriers had strafed and bombed Japanese airfields and installations, and one of the highlights in the operations had been an aerial duel between a Hellcat, piloted by a New Zealander, and a Jap ace. The naval observer wrote a vivid account of dogfights in which Hellcats providing fighter cover for the Task Force battled against Japanese aircraft.

Other writers who contributed articles on naval matters to service publications were Cyril Falls and Cdr. Anthony Kimmins, R.N., whose article on how in 1944 minesweepers in the Scheldt had swept clear

133

The exploits of a group of Commandos were reported in this story from an Australian service newspaper.

23 COMMANDOS LIVED ON JAPANESE BASE

A remarkable exploit by an Australian Commando detachment left on Jap-held Bougainville. They defied capture to send a stream of intelligence by radio

ILLUSTRATION BY F. N. KENT

WITH the disclosure that Australian troops taken over from the Americans in Bougain some of the story may now be told of the magnifi commando work carried out on the island by f than 30 men during the dark days of revers 1942.

These men spent 19 months on the island be it was possible to give them relief. During time they established watching posts in half a d areas, reported by wireless every move the Japa made in those areas, carried out demolitions made countless reconnaissances.

Their history can be summarised as follows:

It was impossible to reinforce them;

They suffered no battle casualties, but every contracted malaria;

They could receive Army rations for about ha their stay; for the remainder they had to subsis the country;

They managed to escape actual detection, their posts were never over-run during occupanc

seventy miles of mine-strewn water that lay between Allied convoys and the vital port of Antwerp, was read by thousands of servicemen in Europe, South-East Asia, and the Pacific.

An account of the experiences of an American, Sam Adkins, sailing across the North Atlantic in an L S T (Landing Ship Tank) appeared in several Allied service publications in the middle of 1945. Adkins had lived in Louisville, Kentucky, just across the Ohio River from where the craft had been built, and had actually seen the keel laid and watched the ship being built. He sailed on board the L S T from America to Canada and then continued in convoy to Europe. It had been truly a pioneer voyage. No man aboard had ever been more than a few miles to sea in an L S T, and nobody had any idea how the boat would act in the Atlantic. The L S T was a five-thousand-ton vessel, flat-bottomed with practically no keel and no rolling chocks to hold her steady.

Operations by all branches of the Allied air forces were reported by ground personnel or aircrews and by war correspondents. Stories about fighters, bombers, air-transports, flying boats, and air-sea rescue, by such notable writers as Flt. Lt. S. M. Lyndale and Sqn. Ldr. E. Michael Salzar, appeared regularly in service publications. On 31 December 1943, John Hope started a new feature in *Union Jack* especially for the R.A.F. 'about those who fly and those who keep 'em flying'.

An article by Lawrence Wilkinson that appeared in several service publications told the story of the day in Amiens gaol when, in February 1944, Group Captain 'F for Freddie' Pickard had died leading a formation of Mosquitos on a 'Pimpernel job'. With precision bombing the Mosquitos had blasted a hole in the prison walls to enable French prisoners of the Gestapo to escape with important information for the Allies.

Murray Smith, an air observer, wrote a first-rate account of a daylight raid on Brandenburg by a thousand Fortresses in which he had been one of the ten thousand airmen taking part. Soldiers reading accounts of massive bomber raids such as this always marvelled at the thought of a whole division of ten thousand men flying over an enemy city at one time.

Leslie Kark, a writer well known to service readers, told the epic story of the last sortie of the Stirling bomber 'H' for Harry. The crew of eight had been detailed for a low-level attack on the Fiat works in Turin, a task necessitating two separate climbs over the Swiss Alps. The pilot of the aircraft was Flight Sergeant Middleton, who had been a sheep-farmer in Australia. Despite the fact that the aircraft was sluggish in gaining height for the outward crossing of the Alps, the pilot persevered on his perilous course, flying through a pass to bomb his target. The Stirling was hit repeatedly as she flew low through heavy flak. A burst between the pilot and the second pilot sent the bomber into a dive. Middleton had been badly hit but he took control. Other members of the crew were wounded, but they

135

stuck to their posts as their captain set course for home. Middleton's wounds were appalling: his left hand was injured, his left leg mangled, his right eye smashed in and the whole bone above it exposed. Yet he brought the Stirling back through the Alpine pass and across France, dodging searchlights and flak, until, over England, with five minutes' petrol left, he ordered the crew to bale out. When the last man had dropped from the aircraft, Middleton headed the crippled plane out to sea rather than risk hitting a town or village. It crashed two miles off the coast. Murray Smith concluded the moving story:

> Above the grave of this sheep-farmer, who has been called perhaps the greatest captain of aircraft under whom any crew has ever had the honour to serve, they have erected a small wooden cross, painted white: the inscription says, quite briefly, 'Flight Sergt. R. H. Middleton, V.C. Royal Australian Air Force.'

Stories from Australian service papers were reprinted in other service periodicals, and Allied troops, particularly those in South-East Asia, were able to follow the progress of the Australians in the Pacific. With the news that Australian troops had taken over from the Americans in Bougainville in the Solomon Islands came the story of twenty-three Australian soldiers who had been left behind on the island when it was first overrun by the Japanese in 1941. For nineteen months this commando detachment had continued to operate, establishing watching posts in half a dozen areas, reporting Japanese movements by radio, and carrying out demolitions.

With the nearest Allied base six hundred miles away, the Australians had carried on their valuable work, living off the land on taro, sweet potatoes, birds, pigs, and, occasionally, meat from cattle sneaked from a plantation. This story appeared in the Australian and American general press and was reprinted in British and American service publications. The Americans acknowledged the services rendered by the Australian force by decorating seven of their number. The article was a reminder to British servicemen in Europe and the Middle East that the Australians, who had served in the Middle East before their recall to face the Japanese threat to their homeland, were still in the war up to their necks, in the jungles of New Guinea and the islands of the South Pacific.

Servicemen often found themselves stationed or on furlough in towns and cities they might have heard about but had never dreamt they would ever see, and they liked to read about the various places they had visited or were likely to visit. Thousands of men visited Cairo, Alexandria, Ismailia, Tel Aviv, Nairobi, Baghdad, Bombay, Calcutta, and Colombo. Servicemen were familiar with Crawford Market Bazaar in Bombay although it was out of bounds, with the bedlam of Chandni Chauk in Delhi, and the Chowringhee, Calcutta. What serviceman who had been to Cairo had not heard of Shepheards? Who had never heard of the transit camp at Deolali or the hill stations of Poona, Simla, and Murree? Who had never had a cup of char at the Shandy Tavern or the Services Bath-Canteen, Ballard Pier, Bombay? What American serviceman had not heard of Rainbow Corner in Piccadilly? Then there were Naples, Rome, Paris, and Brussels, not to mention Teheran, Algiers, and Tunis.

In an interesting article entitled 'The Middle East Pattern' which was published in *Jambo* at the beginning of 1944, Capt. J. O'Neil Pearson gave his impressions of various cities in Egypt, Palestine, Lebanon, and Syria after having spent three years in East Africa. He reported that the traffic in Cairo was frightening, that there was no lack of luxury goods, and that the bookshelves were a revelation after the starved bookshelves of Nairobi. He said that Shepheards' famous terrace, during the week he was there, was monopolized by a noisy party from America, among whom were Jack Benny, Dinah Shore and Anna Lee. Another day it had been Noël Coward and Josephine Baker. All were in Egypt to entertain the troops.

George Gumption   **No. 1 — George Arrives**

George Gumption cartoon from *The Crusader*.

At that time the Eighth Army was on the other side of the Mediterranean, but O'Neil Pearson said that the Crusader insignia was still very much in evidence, as were the shoulder flashes of the fighting divisions such as the 4th Indian and the Highland Division. Pearson complained that the train to Palestine compared unfavourably with the K.U.R. He had to scramble for a seat and there was no restaurant car (officers did not like to have to scramble for a seat or travel without a restaurant car), but at Qantara and Gaza, E.F.I. canteens served hot meals. For Captain Pearson, the impressive thing about Palestine was its smallness. Food was poor and rationed, only citrus fruits being plentiful in season. The Jews, by their ability and technical skill, had raised great industries out of the desert sands, but Captain Pearson thought that Tel Aviv was not their happiest effort: it was a jumble of ultra-modern concrete slabs with a Coney Island seafront and a Brighton beach, full of cafés, cabarets, and joints, 'gals', 'popsies', and bints. Amusing and bawdy, it was a Mecca for soldiers on leave.

Despite the dirt and squalor and the unheeding polygot multitudes of Jerusalem Captain Pearson felt a sense of tradition and security in the Holy City. He was far more impressed by Beirut, which had the appearance of a French Riviera town and where the hotels were civilized, the cuisine French, the local wine as warm and mature as the women. He found the enclosed streets of the Souk in Damascus fascinating, watching craftsmen at work – leather workers, engravers, silver- and goldsmiths, carpenters, weavers, and glass blowers. It was a good place for bargains, for soldiers with the right bargaining counters such as guns, ammunition, and hashish.

And the last word from *Soldier*.

"And what's your release group?"

For interested servicemen, there were often informative articles on the development of Allied resources and the possibilities for post-war growth. An eye-opener for most readers was 'Britain strikes oil' by Michael Mason, reprinted in *Ceylon Review* on 18 November 1944. The article started with a quotation from a British politician speaking in 1918 when the subject of British oil possibilities had come up for discussion: 'I'll drink every pint of oil you can find in Britain.' Commented Mason, 'Had he been alive today he would be drinking something like 26,000,000 gallons a year, enough to make any politician realise the dreadful consequences of having to swallow his words.' At the time of Mason's article there were 238 producing wells in Britain. Mason mentioned the Petroleum (Production) Act placed in the Statute Book in 1933 which, among other things, nationalized oil so that it could only be worked under license. He also stated that, early in 1943, American drilling contractors had arrived in Britain to assist in the drilling.

An article by George Murray reprinted in *Ceylon Review* on 2 December 1944 commented on *Tomorrow's Children*, published by the Tory Reform Committee, which asserted that Britain must have more children to preserve her greatness. The Tory pamphlet suggested that one way to redress the balance of population would be to adopt an immigration policy similar to those of the Dominions and America and to bring in Italians, Bulgarians, Poles, and Russians in order to maintain the nation. Said Murray: 'To adopt deliberately a policy of immigration into this intensively settled country would be a fearful confession of racial defeat. It is not, of course, advocated in the Tory Reform pamphlet, but is mentioned as one of the three choices which lie before us.'

A few weeks previously an article released to service papers 'Australia Might have a job for you', discussed Australia's potential as a land of post-war settlement for British servicemen and stated that reconstruction, national works, and new industries were going to need new and more labour, and that there was still room down on the farm.

'Emigration is not escapism', by a writer who had lived in South Africa, criticized another writer, John L. Wooton, who had 'Threatened wholesale evacuation of the U.K. to the sunlit lands overseas'. Yet another article on emigration, this one by Emmanuel Shinwell and entitled 'An Empire Sacrifice that Must be Made', posed the question 'Can Britain people the Empire alone?' Shinwell declared that Britain's own needs would be great, but she would have to make a sacrifice to populate the Dominions and there was an urgent need for sound emigration policy.

By and large, the vast majority of servicemen, civilians in uniform, were no more influenced by service newspapers than they had been by the non-service press. They appreciated information and enjoyed various features. They read the views of others, interpreting ideas as it suited them and groused and grumbled or approved accordingly. Seasoned servicemen irreverently referred to newspapers as 'the comics' or 'the funny papers' – but there were very few servicemen who did not read them.